THE WISH BOOKLET

VOLUME III

Fashion 1871 - 1875

By Susan Bonsall Sirkis

Copyright 1975, by Susan Bonsall Sirkis

All rights reserved. No part of this booklet may be reproduced without permission of the author.

ISBN 0-913786-03-9

Helen Barglebaugh's antique doll, Carolyne Milholland's wax, and Rosamond McCall's reproduction --all costumed using patterns in this booklet.

## THE WISH BOOKLET

A few years ago, I wrote an article about French Fashion Dolls which appeared in the pages of the TOY TRADER. At that time, I did a great deal of research and I learned a lot about these little charmers. I also began to wish for a Fashion Doll of my own. I wished hard enough and voila --finally she appeared. There are many fine reproductions on the market today, and the patterns in this booklet were created for one of them.

Volume I in this series covers the middle Victorian period; Volume II covers the early Victorians. This present booklet covers the later period. This is not Victorian in its final years, but it is close. It required only the tight dropped bustle and other upholstery of the 80's to bring to an end the period during which women resembled pincushions more than anything else. They were graceful pincushions and an ornament to their time. A small head, set upon a graceful neck and shoulders, a full bust, tiny waist, and small hands and feet were the desirable feminine form upon which was hung the bustle. Women bent slightly forward at the waist in order to balance that object, and as the bustle grew, it became fashionable to wear more and more hair piled on the head, again, as a balancing element.

All of the dresses in this book may be mixed and matched --one tunic with another top, or a top and skirt without the tunic. Using the patterns given here, you ought to be able to study any fashion plate of the period and by varying trims and analyzing drapes, you should be able to make up any dress. It is recommended that you read the entire booklet before commencing to make any of the dresses.

Many of the clothes and accessories in this booklet were copied directly from actual items loaned to me by Helen Barglebaugh who, in turn, borrowed them from a very distinguished French Fashion Doll who lives with her.

These patterns will fit the dolls in the previous two booklets and also the one given here, or any doll of the ten to twelve inch size. You should work the basic patterns out in muslin first, of course, to make the minor alterations necessitated by the different types of doll bodies. As always, your own patience is your only limitation. I believe in wishes -- if you dream, it may happen. If you wish, you can work at making your wish come true, and reap the rewards.

This is the third in a series of these booklets -- I have never dedicated one before. Now I shall:

To all collectors and creators, to those who encourage, to those who wish and achieve their wishes, this booklet is lovingly dedicated.

West Point, New York  Susan Sirkis
April 1967

## FRENCH FASHION DOLL BODY

The Fashion Dolls all seem to have the same type of body. There are some variations in cut but the finished effect is similar. I believe that these bodies were constructed to resemble the human female form as it appeared when clothed. Hence, we have the long slender waist and legs; the high bust; the tiny feet and hands demanded by the fashionable silhouette of the day. The slightly disjointed and protruding derriere in doll form is even represented. In the human form, of course, these anatomical intricricies were achieved by the use of corsets, bust improvers, and bustles.

The Fashion Doll bodies that I have seen were all of kid. The hands were also of kid, although I see no reason why you may not substitute porcelin hands if you wish. The smaller dolls have mitten hands and the larger ones have the fingers either stitched, or separated. Because the mitten hands are more common in the small size, the pattern for the body has that type.

The seam allowance on the body pattern, you will notice, is narrower than I usually show. These pieces must be placed, right sides together and whipped, rather than stitched together. If you have a zig-zag machine, try that. Otherwise, do it by hand, with small close stitches. First, stitch together both back leg seams. Then sew the toe pieces in place to the legs. Then sew the soles to the legs. Turn carefully and sew the crotch seam. Sew the side seams of the body. Sew the body to the legs at waist line. Sew each arm piece together. Turn and stuff to dotted line. Place a dab (and to quote "a little dab'll do you") inside the top of the arm and glue to seal the saw-dust in. Stuff the legs to the waist line. Cut the pattern pieces marked "inner body" of a firm material such as muslin or percale. Seam together by machine. Stuff tightly and sew bottom together. Stuff legs to a little above the waistline. Slip the already stuffed inner body inside the kid body. The inner body should fit tightly. If it does not, open the top seam a little and add more stuffing. Glue the arms to the under side of the head. Glue the head to the top of the inner body. Pull the kid up over the porcelin and whip the shoulders closed. Slip a little dabble of glue underneath the kid, at center front and back and at each shoulder. This will hold the head in place. Push the little flaps of the body (at the side seams) underneath the arms.

Although I have used kid and sawdust as materials for the making of the body, you may wish to use muslin and cotton if the other is unavailable. You can get the sawdust for free at your local lumber store - you should sift it to remove the big pieces. If you use kid, practice sewing on a scrap before you start on the body. Use a small sharp needle and develop a good technique before you start the real thing.

## WIGS AND HAIR-DOS

      Since the French Fashion Doll is habitually bald, it is necessary to make a wig for her. It is possible, of course, to weave a human hair wig for her, or to purchase one. This, however, is the method which I have found to be the best for me, and for the effect. It is sort of a cross between the method used by the Japanese doll makers and the method used here in the United States. Start by getting a cork to fit in the hole at the top of the head. Whittle it down so that the top of the head will be rounded, like a head should be. Then, cover the top of the head with a piece of foil paper smashed down as smoothly as possible. This foil should extend down over the face and neck. It is to protect the head while you are molding the base upon which to make the wig. For this base you may use either buckram or muslin. If you use buckram, all you have to do is wet it in warm water. Smooth it down over the head and onto the neck and face. Tie string around it to hold it in place. If you use muslin, you will have to dip it in a mixture of 1/2 water and 1/2 Elmer's Glue-All. Then proceed as with buckram. After the wig base is completely dry, untie the string and remove the foil from the head. You will have to pull the foil off of the wig base, so be sure to get it all off. Slip the wig base back on the head and mark the hair line. Cut on this line, and check again to make sure that you have the hair line you want. Next, take a piece of the hair material (real hair, straightened mohair, or whatever) and brush it out so that it is smooth and fairly even. Hold it between your forefinger and third finger and trim the edge to get a straight line. Place some glue on the underside of the wig in the front. Glue the hair in place. Until you have made several wigs like this you'd better do it in three small pieces - first the two temples, then the top. For the long back hair, sew the wig material between two pieces of tissue paper on your machine. Pull the tissue paper away and glue as shown in the picture. The bottom row should be glued to the under side of the wig, in case you wish to make an upswept hair-do. For the center part, sew two of these strips together, divide and glue to the front of the head. When you arrange the hair, pull the front hair over the ends. Now you can arrange the hair as shown throughout the booklet, using small stitches of matching thread to hold it in place. An alternative method is to glue the front hair directly onto the doll, in the direction in which hair grows - that is to say, back. If you want to do this, trim a little of the wig base back. This method requires considerable dexterity and skill, so practice on an old doll first. This is the most natural appearing, since the hair does appear to be growing right out of the head. If any little wisps escape the glue, they can be trimmed off with a pair of manicure scissors.

      I make my curls by winding the hair in strands over toothpicks or knitting needles, or anything round and thin, wetting, and drying. For bangs and front curls, I make the curls separately and glue them on at the hairline. It is almost impossible to tell that they are glued on and the glue holds the curl almost indefinitely.

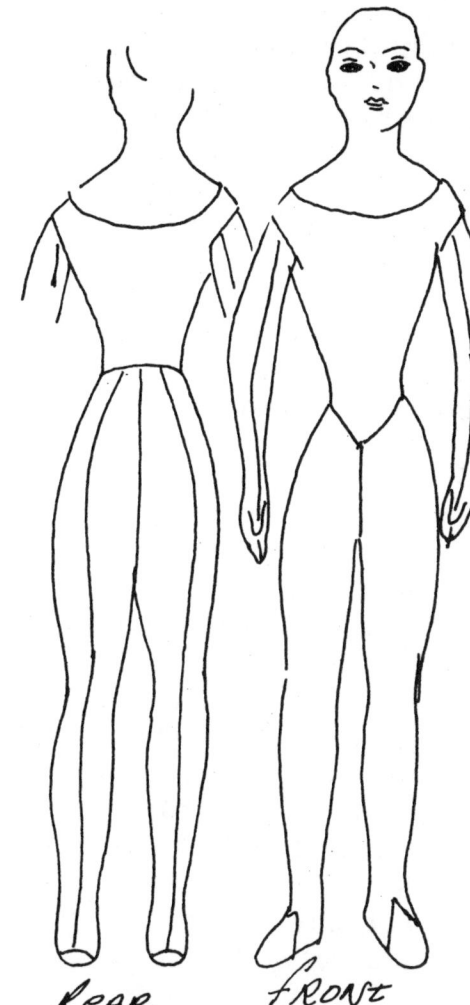

Rear    Front

French Fashion Doll Body

Inner body with head glued on. Arms are glued to the head

Hair, arranged in a pouf of large curls. Follow directions in Vol. II for making hair pieces

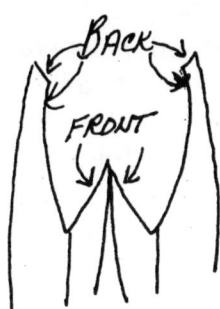

Legs, before crotch seam is sewn. Sew fronts to fronts & backs to backs. Then sew to torso at waist.

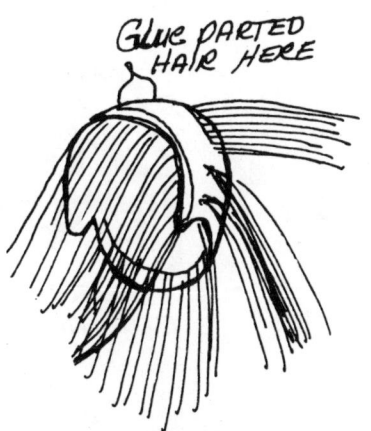

Glue parted hair here

Wig base, showing places to attach hair

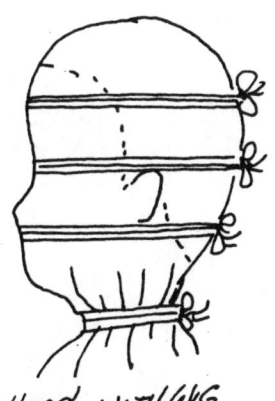

Head, with carved cork in place

Head, with wig base material tied in place to dry. Dotted lines show where to cut away excess.

Wig with front hair glued directly on doll - note base is cut back from front

# LINGERIE

The wardrobe of the French Fashion Doll contained many sets of matched underwear. Each set contained a chemise, drawers, one or two petticoats, and a sort of loose blouse, or combing jacket. In addition, the wardrobes had a nightgown and wrapper, a few flannel petticoats, a bustle or two, and a set of corsets. Each item was superbly and professionally made, and made usually by machine. The use of the sewing machine had become widespread by the late 1860's and by the seventies women were using it to advantage to create all the fancy ruffles and tucks fashion demanded. The earlier chain stitch was replaced by the development of the lock stitch. Hence, you may use your machine on all of the patterns given. Use a very fine needle and fine thread. Adjust the machine so that the stitch length is very short.

Make as many, or as few, of these sets as you have time and patience for. Use batiste and eyelet or baby val for the ruffles and trims. Only very infrequently does baby Val appear on the original garments. Cotton eyelet however, is becoming increasingly difficult to find and you may find the substitution not only preferable but mandatory.

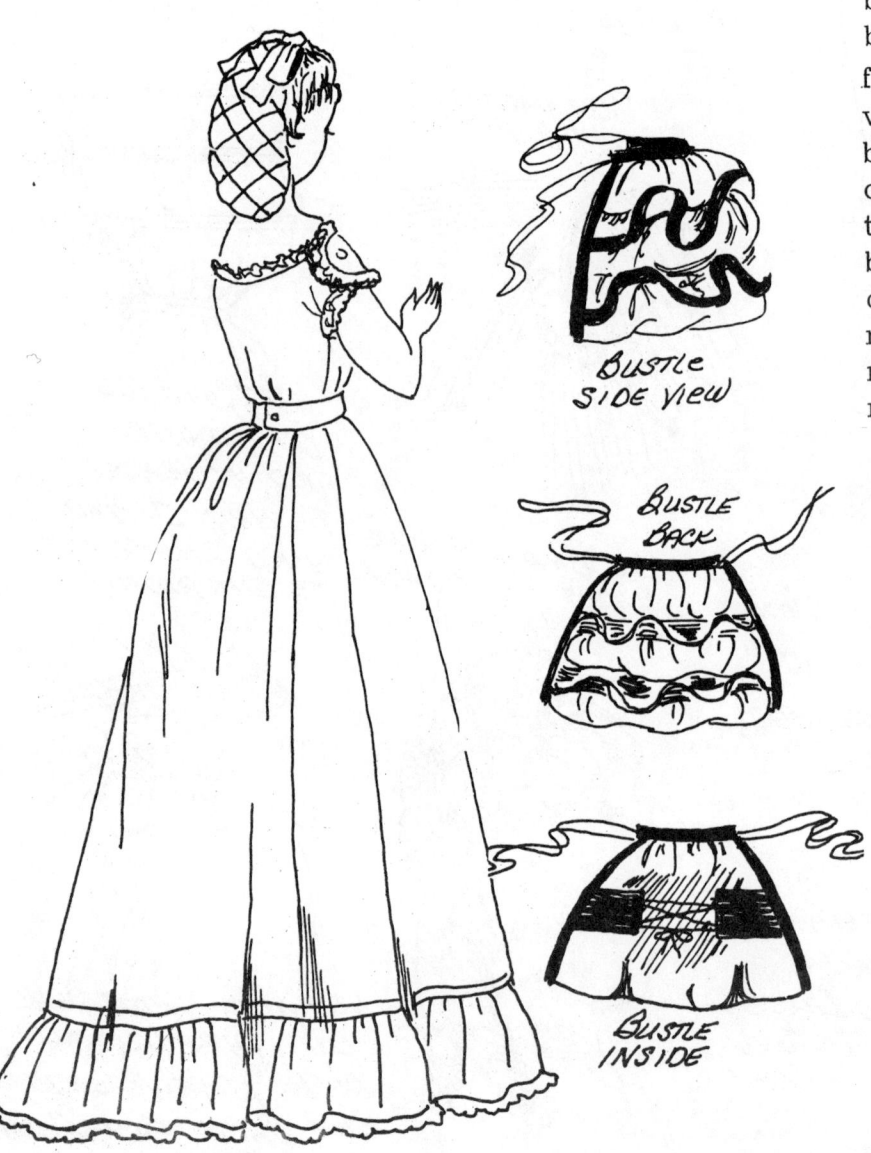

#1 - CHEMISE. Cut pieces of lace insertion to the lengths shown on pattern. First baste in place, to the outside on the front only. Then whip a narrow lace ruffle to the outer edges of each piece, catching the batiste and the insertion with each stitch. Cut the fabric away from the insertion on the underside, turn the raw edges under and whip those down to the insertion. Next French seam the two underarm seams together. In all of this lingerie, the French seams are as narrow as possible. Cut a narrow length of bias binding and bind all top edges. Make two small buttonholes as marked in the front. Sew the corresponding buttons to the back. Whip a narrow lace ruffle all around the neck and sleeves. Hem bottom.

#2 - <u>OPEN DRAWERS.</u> Make hems in bottoms. Make small tucks on solid lines. Trim bottoms with 1/2" ruffles of self material trimmed with narrow lace. So that the ruffles will not be too wide, they should be cut to 1/2", and narrowly hemmed. Whip the lace to the ruffle. Then gather the top edge and sew in place. Sew seam BC on each leg. Hem edges AB on each leg. Run a gathering thread through tops and draw up to fit waist. Sew to a waist band and close in back with button and button hole.

#3 - <u>CORSET.</u> Make the corset of light weight linen. Use pipe cleaners for stays. Sew center back seam. Slash on indicated lines and sew the six gussets in place. Using narrow strips of the linen, make the casings for the bones on the shaded areas. For the front casings, stitch the wide front hem on the outside edges of the shaded areas. Work the five eyelets on each side. Insert the "bones" and work scallops around top and bottom with button hole stitch. Lace up the front with narrow cotton tape, ribbon, or embroidery floss. NOTE: So that there will be no raw edges on the inside of the garmet, baste the gussets in place. Top stitch on the right side, and whip the raw edges to the underside.

#4 - <u>FLANNEL PETTICOAT.</u> Use a piece of fine wool flannel. Cut it 10" by 6 1/2". Sew up center back seam leaving about 1 1/2" open at top. Make two 1/4" tucks about 1" from the bottom. Buttonhole stitch the scallops around the bottom. Use a nickle to trace around to get the proper size. Hem placket opening and gather top to fit doll. Sew to a waistband of batiste. Close with button and buttonhole.

#5 - <u>STOCKINGS.</u> Although Madame Demorest, in her fashion magazine for October 1875, announced that she saw no reason why a lady of refined task should "dress her limbs in the attire of ballet dancers.... to stimulate and encourage the ribald conduct of men who watch..... at the Church steps" my Fashion Doll has some pink and white stripped stockings which I fabricated of some of my daughter's cast-offs. When Madame lowered the boom on them, stripped stockings had been a fad for two years; in spite of her they remained fashionable for another few. However, white stockings were always considered in the best of taste. At any rate, use children's cotton socks. Place the pattern on them so that the top of the pattern is at the ribbed top of the sock. Sew the back seam. Sew the sole in place with tiny over cast stitches.

#6 - <u>BUSTLE.</u> The original bustle was made of something very nearly like horsehair, bound with blue cotton satin. You might want to use crinoline, muslin, or a starched lace. Fold the base on solid line. Baste around edges. Make small box pleats in bottom pouf. Matching the dotted lines, sew to line A. Fold up on dotted lines and baste top to dotted line B. Make small box pleats in top pouf. Sew to dotted line B, catching the top of the lower pouf. Baste to top of bustle. Cut the two lacing pieces of the binding material. Hem them and baste in place as shown on bustle base. Bind the two ruffles of the poufs. Bind the sides of the bustle, catching all edges of the poufs, and the top and bottom of the bustle. Gather the top of the bustle to 1 1/2" and bind. Sew cotton or ribbon tapes to either side for waist ties. Punch holes as indicated on lacing base. Lace with ribbon and draw up so that bustle does not flatten out over doll's derriere.

#7 - <u>PETTICOAT.</u> Make of batiste. French seam the side gores to the front gores, the back gores to the side gores. Seam center back seam together as far as dot. Hem above dot for placket. Sew hem in bottom. To solid line, sew a ruffle of batiste edged with narrow lace. Gather back gores on dotted lines and draw up to fit doll's waist. Mount on a waist band and close with button and button hole. A second petticoat may be made for each set of underwear by the same pattern, cut just a little fuller at the bottom.

#8 - <u>WRAPPER.</u> Make of light weight linen or batiste. Sew shoulder seams. Turn back front facings and hem in place. Cut a piece of fabric about 1/2" wide and long enough to reach the bottom of the wrapper. Turn under a narrow seam on each side and baste in place up the front of the right side on top of the ruffle. (Make a ruffle, 1/2" wide, either of self material or lace. Baste it up the right front edge and around the neck to the right side.) Stitch a 1/2" band in place covering raw edges down the front. Sew buttons to left side and work corresponding buttonholes on right side. Cut a narrow piece of bias binding long enough to go around neck and stitch around neck, with the right side of the binding on the right side of the ruffle. Turn the binding down and stitch the other side to the wrapper, thus concealing the raw edges. French seam the underarm seam together. Turn a narrow hem in bottom. Sew the upper part of each sleeve to the lower part. Trim the bottom with a ruffle, and bind the raw edge, this time on the underside. Set the sleeves in the armcyes with a narrow felled seam.

#9 - <u>NIGHTGOWN.</u> Make the nightgown by the wrapper pattern of batiste and directions, except omitting the band and ruffles. Instead, finish all edges (except the bottom which should be hemmed) with a small scallop worked in buttonhole stitch.

#10 - <u>COMBING JACKET.</u> Made of fine linen or batiste. Baste insertion in place down both fronts. Turn facings up and with a narrow hem, stitch down over edge of insertion. Cut fabric away from that edge of insertion. Make a narrow hem in the other side and whip insertion in place. Sew center back seam and shoulder seams. Sew the two collar pieces together along the outside edges. Clip seams, turn, and press. Sew to neck of jacket. Face the edges on the inside with a narrow bias band. Use wrapper sleeve pattern. Sew upper to lower sleeves. Face bottom of sleeve with narrow bias band. Sew underarm seams. Set sleeves in armcyes. Face bottom of jacket with narrow bias band. Sew tiny buttons to x's on left front and work corresponding buttonholes to right front. Whip a narrow lace ruffle around collar, down right front, around bottom, and at bottom of sleeves.

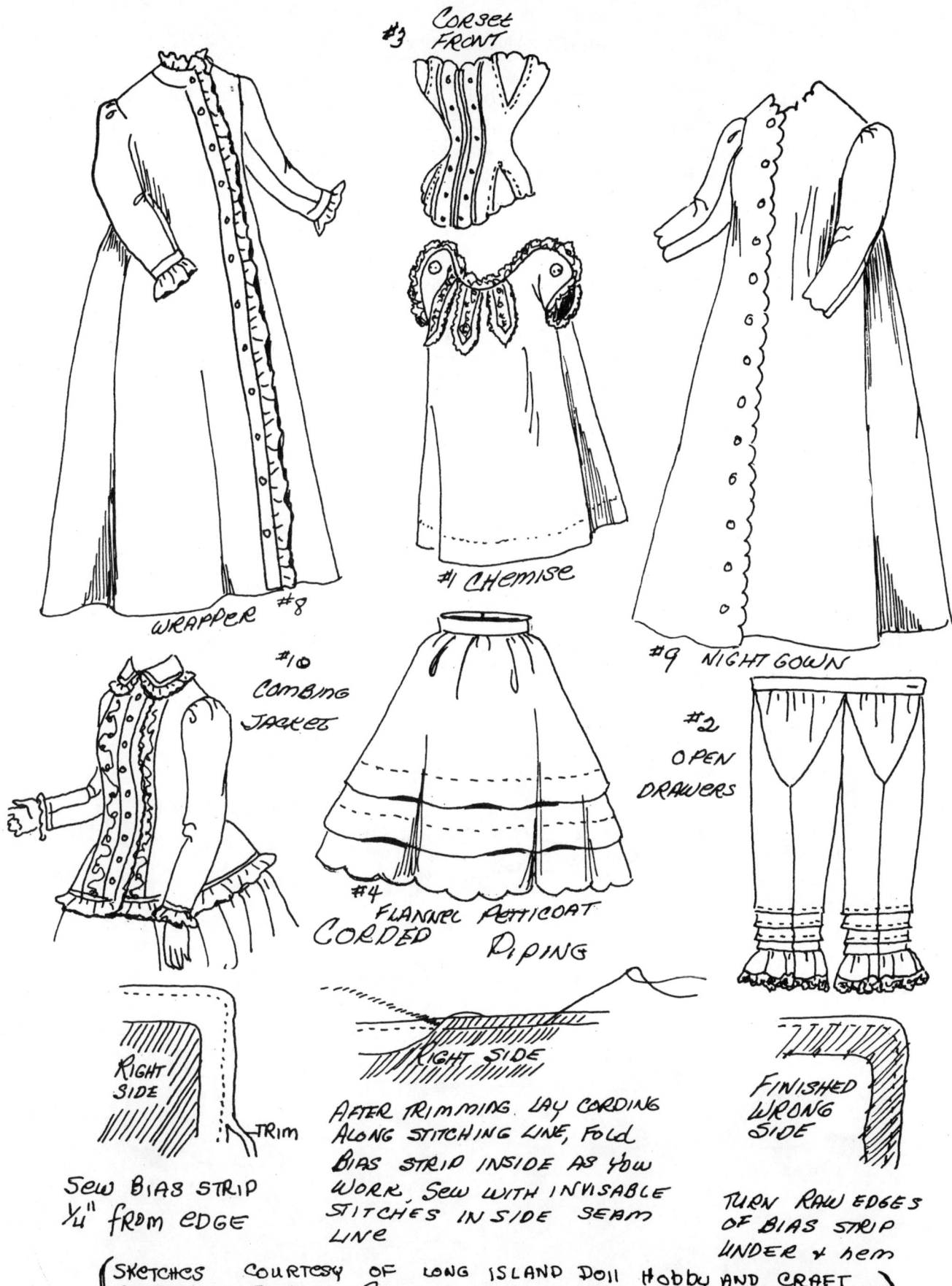

## SHOES AND BOOTS

#11 - <u>BOOTS</u>. Use thin slightly stiff leather in either brown, black or a color to harmonize with the outfit. Sew flap to inside boot side piece, using tiny overcast stitches. Sew back seam. With an E-xacto knife or razor blade, cut buttonholes in flap and reinforce the holes from the back with a dab of Elmer's Glue-All. Sew front seam below flap. Glue the leather outer sole on top of the cardboard sole. Actually, on the outside of the shoe. Sew tiny metal buttons or beads up the side for buttons. Carve the heels of Balsa or some other soft wood. Paint black with model airplane dope, or another type of shiny paint. Glue to heel of boot.

#12 - <u>SHOES</u>. Make of thin slightly stiff leather or fabric. If you use fabric, glue it to a piece of paper first, and then make the same as you would the leather. Use a matching or contrasting color to the outfit. Sew the center back seam. Glue to the leather inner sole. Glue the leather outer sole to the inner one. Make the heels according to the directions given under Boots.

-10-

## THE DRESSES

#13 - <u>PLEATER</u>. You will have, no doubt, noticed that the dresses and skirts of this period are profusely trimmed with ruffles and pleats. While the pleats can be made by hand, it is a long drawn out process and the results are not so professional as those made with mechanical aid. If you have an old pleater, you are in good shape. However, most of us do not have one of the old ones and are forced to seek other means. The pleater which I made works very well and can be made easily. Get a board about 2 feet long, one or two inches thick, and about two or three inches wide. Measuring carefully, draw lines across the top every 1/4". On either side, at each of these lines, drive a nail into the wood. Twist a piece of wire around the top nail, cross over the board and wrap it around the first and second nail, bring it back to the first side and wrap it around the next two nails, and so on until the whole board has been covered on the lines you penciled in. There is your pleater. To make a gauge to determine the size of the pleat, you will need a piece of flat metal. I used a Dritz measure - one of the little black ones with the slot down the middle. I cut the top and bottom off and used one side of the measure. To prepare the fabric for pleating, cut a long strip, about 1 and 1/2" wide. Machine stitch a narrow hem along one edge. Press. Pull the strip of material all the way through your pleater, under the wires. Slide the gauge between the first and second wires and under the material. Pull the material up the width of the gauge. Remove the gauge and insert it in the next place. Repeat until your whole board is covered with a series of even loops. Then press the loops all over in one direction. Remove that portion from the pleater after the fabric has set and machine stitch along the top in the direction of the pleats. Repeat until you have made a strip of pleating as long as you think you will need.

#14 - <u>THE SKIRT</u>. Most of the dresses in the Booklet are two pieces and have the same skirt pattern. The skirt itself is easy to make and only the applied trimming is time consuming. The pattern is given here and the trims are discussed under the individual dresses. Sew the center back seam. Make a casing of a bias strip of self fabric and sew, on wrong side, to lines indicated on pattern. Make your stitches small so

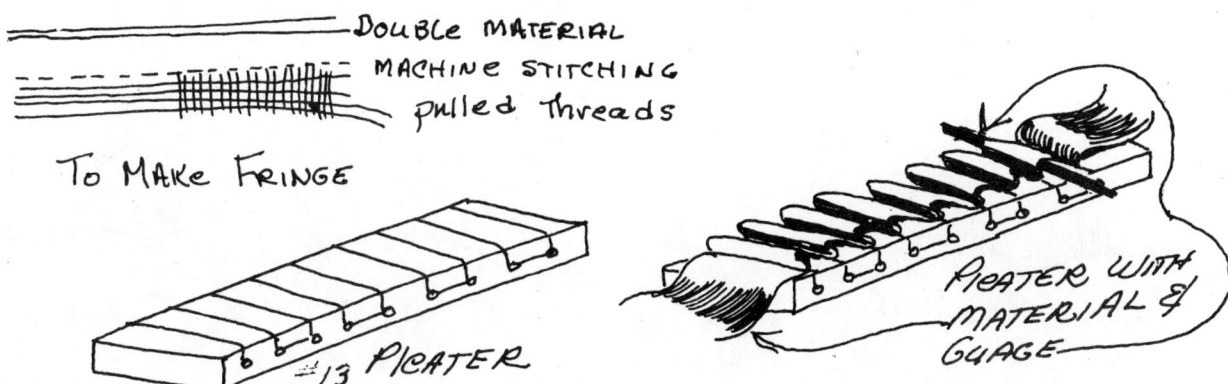

that they will not show on the right side of the fabric. Fasten a tape to each side seam, and run towards the center, bringing them out at center back. Sew the two side gores to the front and then sew the sides to the back. Cut a piece of cotton satin, on the straight of the material about 1 1/2" wide. With right sides together, sew it around the bottom of the skirt. Turn, press. Turn the bottom of the skirt up to the hem line. Run a gathering thread around the top of the facing. Draw it up to fit the skirt, and hem the top of the facing to the skirt. Hem the placket opening in the back and gather the top of the back so that the skirt top fits the doll's waist. Sew to a cotton tape waist band, and close with a hook and eye. This is the foundation upon which you will place all the tunics and trims for most of the following dresses. It should always be made this way and then trimmed, as it presents a neater appearance. If you wish, the raw seams of the skirt may be overcast by hand. Should you desire, the back of the skirt may be arranged in box pleats as shown below. If you do that, omit the casing and draw string. In some cases, the design may be applied directly onto the skirt, simulating the tunic. This is especially applicable towards the end of the period.

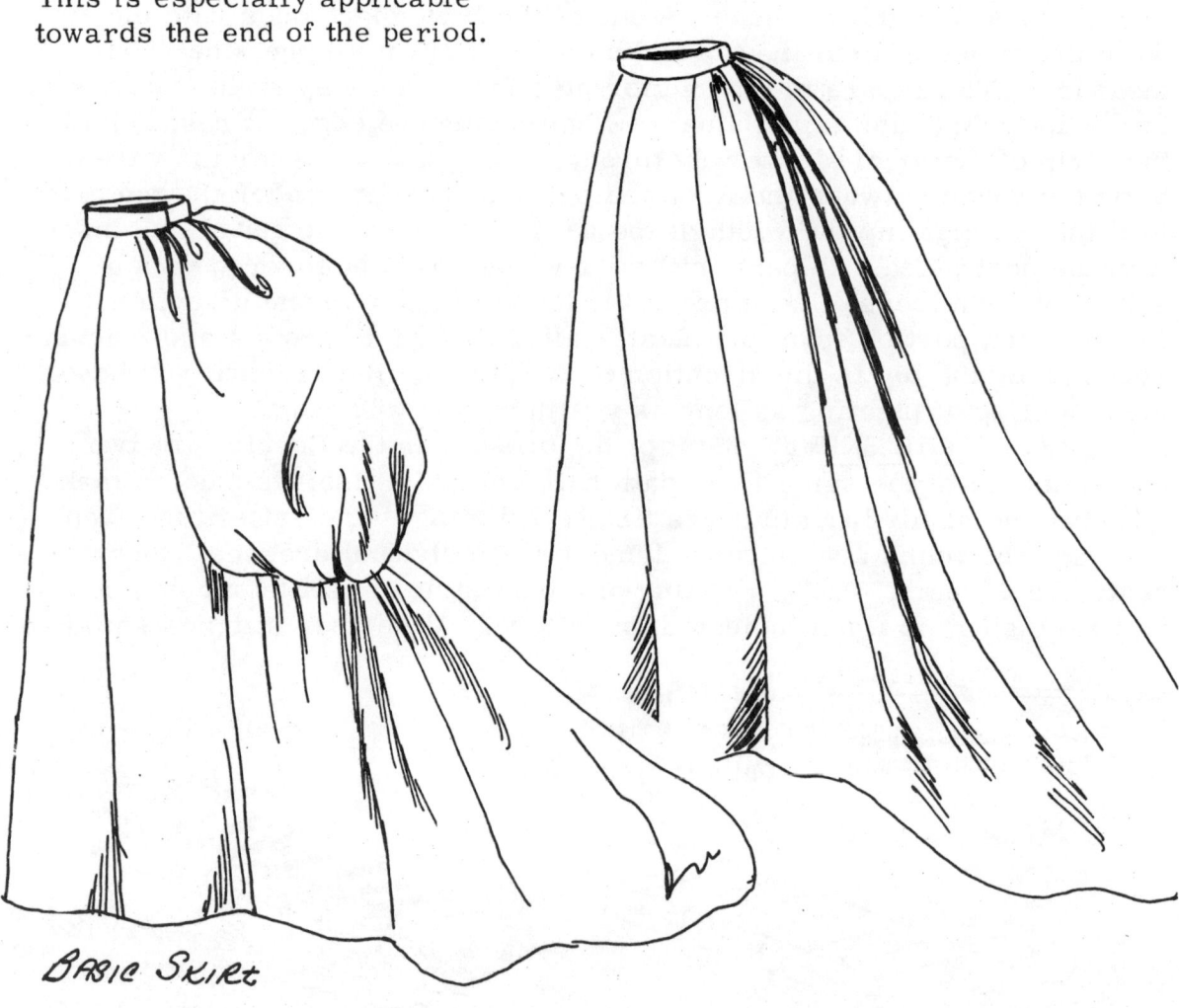

BASIC SKIRT

**#15 - MORNING ROBE.** This pattern may be made up as either a morning dress, or if your doll is very elegant, a wrapper. If you make a wrapper out of it, leave it open all the way down the front. Make of a dark print cotton or linen and line the top portion with white cotton, cut and sewn in one with the dress fabric. The collars, cuffs, and pockets are to be made of harmonizing velvet. Sew the center back seam and the shoulder seams. Whip a narrow hem in the velvet collar and sew to the dress, with the wrong side of the collar against the right side of the dress. Face the raw edges with silk bias binding. Whip a narrow lace ruffle to the facing. Turn a narrow hem in the top of the pockets and baste a narrow seam allowance along the remaining sides. Tack a ribbon loop to the bottom point of the pocket. Whip stitch the pockets in place to the fronts of the dress. Turn the front facing back and hem in place. Sew under arm seams. Sew sleeve uppers to sleeve bottoms. Set sleeves into armcyes. Make a narrow hem in top of cuffs. Sew bottom of cuffs to bottom of sleeves, turn, and whip raw edges of cuffs together. Add a ribbon loop to point of cuff. Sew ribbon loops to the x's on right front. Sew hooks and eyes to dots in front, underneath so they won't show. Slip stitch the fronts together to large dot. Cut a facing of cotton satin. Sew to bottom of dress, right sides together. Turn and hem facing to dress.

Great care should be taken in the finishing of the inside of the dresses in this Booklet. All of the bodices should be lined - the pattern pieces cut and handled as one. All raw edges should be whipped by hand.

#16 - HOME DRESS.  Make this dress of a light weight cotton, such as batiste, line with batiste.  Prepare several yards of pleating about 1/2" wide.  Make the skirt according to skirt directions and trim the bottom with two rows of pleating.

NOTE:  You may substitute lace for the trim on this dress if you wish. Sew the center back seam.  Sew the two side back pieces to the center back pieces.  Make the box pleats in the back by folding under on the dotted line and tacking in place across the center back.  Sew the dart in the fronts.  Sew the shoulder and underarm seams.  Make a narrow piping by cutting a bias strip of the fabric and basting it over either six strand embroidery floss or crochet cotton.  Baste it to the right side of the bottom of the polonaise.  Turn and hem in place.  You must stitch as close as possible to the cording for this to be effective.  Next, turn under the front facing and feather stitch in place.  Sew the center back seam of the collar.  Pipe the outside edges of the collar as you did the bottom of the polonaise.  Trim with the pleating, adjusting the width as in the sketch.  Sew the collar to the right side of the polonaise, bind the

raw edge on the inside and trim with an upstanding strip of the pleating.  Using the Morning Robe sleeve pattern, sew the upper sleeve piece to the lower piece.  Put a piping at the bottom and hem. Trim as shown with two narrow pleatings, edge with piping, and a bow.  Set sleeves in armcyes. Sew concealed hooks and eyes up the front, and trim with small bows as shown.  Sew two wider ribbons, which may be made of the dress material, to the x's on the polonaise front.  Make them long enough to tie the bow in the back.  To a piece of cotton tape long enough to go around the dolls waist, gather the back drape. Trim the bottom of the back drape with piping and pleating to match the bottom of the polonaise.  Tack the cotton tape to the waist of the polonaise in the back, make a narrow hem in each front edge of the tape and close with a hook and eye.  Tack the sides of the back draped to the curved edge of the polonaise and tie the bow over it.

**#17 - AFTERNOON DRESS.** Make the Afternoon Dress of thin dark blue silk. Make the skirt according to the skirt pattern and trim the bottom with a row of bias shirring 3/4" wide and a slightly gathered bias ruffle about 3/4" wide. Trim the bottom of the bias ruffle with a 1/2" pleating. Make the tunic of matching fabric. Sew the two side front gores to the front gore. Sew the back panel to the side gores. Slash the back gore to the dot and make a narrow rolled hem. Turn the seam allowance around the bottom of the tunic up and baste in place. Sew a 1/2" pleating all around the bottom of the tunic. Place a bias band over the top of the pleating. This band should be 1/4" wide. Gather along the double dotted lines in the back and draw up to fit doll's waist. Sew to a narrow cotton tape and close back with a hook and eye. Line the bodice with batiste. Sew the center back seam of the bodice. Sew the side back seams to the back. Sew shoulder and under arm seams. Sew piping to the bottom of the bodice. Turn under front facing and feather stitch in place. Bind the neck with piping and a narrow ruffle of lace. Line the collar with cotton satin. Pipe the outside edges and hem the edges of the piping. Whip blind edge of the collar to the solid line on the bodice pattern. Right sides together. Again, using the Morning Robe sleeve pattern, sew the upper and lower sleeve pieces together. Trim the bottom with a bias band and pleating as you did the tunic bottom, using the same widths. NOTE: You may put cuffs, made the same way as the collar, over the sleeve pleating if you wish. Close the front with hooks and eyes. Make the braid trim up the back, using either standard round braid, available wherever you can find it, or Middy braid, 1/4", rolled and whipped into shape. Make the tassels of raveled material to match the braid. Make a long bias strip, doubled, to make the bows shown in the picture. Ravel the edges to make fringe. Since the end is pointed, thus on the straight of the material you will have no problem pulling the threads.

#18 - <u>WALKING DRESS.</u>  Make of percale or poplin in a dark color.  Make the skirt according to the usual pattern, except cut off the train.  Trim the bottom of the skirt with a 2" pleating, hemmed at both top and bottom.  Sew the bottom pleats in place as shown in the sketch.  Trim with narrow ribbon or middy braid around the top of the pleating, as shown.  Make the darts in the fronts.  Sew the side backs to the back, making the little pleats up shown on each pattern piece.  Turn the back facing under on the dotted line and hem.  Slash the center back to the dot and hem.  Gather the skirt on the double dotted lines to the underside of the bodice and whip in place.  Sew the shoulder and under arm seams.  Using the Wrapper sleeve pattern, sew the sleeves together and set into armcyes.  Pipe the lower edge of the overdress skirt and the neck.  Trim as shown with ribbon to match skirt.  Trim the bottom of sleeve and the neck with a ruffle of narrow lace.  Make the cuffs and

pipe the top and end edges.  Turn the seam allowance in the bottom up and baste in place.  Trim as shown with ribbon.  Whip to the bottom of sleeve with invisible stitches.  Whip the excess at the bottom and ends closed.  Pipe the outside edge of the bustle trim and put the ribbon on as shown in sketch.  Gather along the double dotted lines and draw up to 1 1/2".  Whip to the edge of a piece of ribbon.  After the dress is on the doll, close the front of the belt with either a bow or small buckle.  Close the back with concealed hooks and eyes.  Trim as shown with either fringe or lace.  The dress is shown worn with the Jabot, #30.  To make fringe, if you don't have any available, cut even lengths of the material along the straight of the goods.  Sew two lengths together with short stitches.  Pull the threads until you have reached the row of stitching.  Trim the top of the material and sew to under **side** of garment.  Though most of the dresses in this Booklet are described in one color, a combination of colors and fabrics was popular during this period.

Delicately colored small florals were worn, and an occasional stripe is seen.

# 19 - <u>VISITING DRESS.</u>  Make this one of black silk, or in a deep shade of green.  Make the skirt according to the skirt directions.  Trim the bottom with a 1 and 1/2" bias strip.  Trim the bottom of the strip with a 1/2" pleating.  About every inch, make two pleats in the bias strip.  Sew the trim to the skirt only at these pleats.  Make a little bias fold of the material and blind stitch over the stitches forming the pleats.  Make a 1/2" pleating of batiste edged with narrow lace and sew to the underside of the skirt hem in the back.  (See Sketch)  The bodice is made by the same pattern and according to the same direction given for #17, the Afternoon Dress.  Omit the bias fold over the pleating at the bottom of the sleeves and add a narrow pleating around the neck in lieu of the cording.  Place the lace ruffle on the inside of the pleating around the neck, and add one to the underside of the sleeve pleating.  Trim with bows tied around the sleeves, at the collar in the front and at the center waist line in the back.  Baste pleats in the backs and front of the tunic.  Sew backs to front as far as bottom pleat.  Pipe the front and backs on solid line.  Trim remainder of backs with 1/2" pleating.  Bring the pleating all the way up to the waist in the back.  Tack the center back together at the pleats.  Gather the top of the back on the double dotted line and draw up to fit doll's waist.  Sew to a cotton tape waist band and close with a hook and eye.

DETAIL OF VISITING DRESS SKIRT TRIM

# 20 - DINNER DRESS.  Make of satin or brocade in a rich color. Make the skirt in the usual manner and leave the skirt plain. Sew the center back seam and the side backs to the center backs. Make the inverted box pleats in the back and whip to underside of back. NOTE: Wherever there are to be these box pleats, do not stitch across the extension when you sew the vertical seam. Sew the darts in the fronts. Turn under the facing on the dotted line and feather stitch in place. Sew the shoulder and under arm seams. Using the Morning Robe sleeve, sew the sleeves together and set into armcyes. Pipe the neck and the sleeve bottoms and the bottom of the bodice in the front. Trim with ribbon or braid as shown, mitreing the trim to achieve the points. The dots represent either small beads or French knots placed closely together. Trim the bottom of the sleeves and the neck and the bottom of the back overskirt with a narrow pleating. Trim the tunic front as shown. Pipe the bottom. Trim bottom with pleating. Make the pleats in the tunic front. Turn under the seam allowance and baste. Whip the tunic front to the front of the skirt at top (waist) and sides only. NOTE: Fringe may be substituted for the pleating.

This dress could also be made in contrasting fabrics, such as silk and velvet. The tablier and plastron (bodice part covered by braid) may be of silk and the rest of velvet. Add jet embroidery, which was very popular, at the sleeves and around the polonaise.

In some patterns in the Booklet, I have made reference to the Morning Robe sleeve pattern. This was omitted because of space. All long sleeves are to be made by the wrapper pattern.

#21 - <u>EVENING DRESS</u>. Use pink or rose silk and line with batiste. Make the skirt according to the directions. Trim the front with a 1 1/2" pleating headed by a narrow lace ruffle. Place a double pleating in the back. Sew a batiste pleating trimmed with lace underneath skirt. Sew center back seams of bodice. Sew side back pieces to backs. Make darts in front and sew shoulder seams. Sew under arm seams. Turn under front facing and feather stitch in place. Pipe and bind the neck line. Trim with a double ruffle of lace, or trim with a doubled edged pleating. Sew the upper and lower sleeve parts together and set sleeves into armcyes. Pipe the lower edge of the sleeves and trim with a 1/2" pleating. Place a 3/4" lace ruffle underneath the pleating on the sleeve bottom. Close the front with concealed hooks and eyes. Trim the center front at the top with a little nosegay of tiny flowers and place matching flowers on each sleeve at the top of the pleating. Sew the side seams on the tunic. Slash to dots and pipe all lower edges. Gather on double dotted lines and draw up as shown in sketch of finished garment. Sew either a lace or a fringe trim at the bottom of the tunic squares. Gather the top and sew to a cotton tape waist band. Pipe the curved edge of the tunic drape and tack it to the waist band in center back. Arrange the folds and tack them to the back edges of the tunic. You may find it necessary to tack the center back closed if it has a tendency to gape open. Place a large bow on the skirt at the bottom points of the drape.

This dress may also be made of net or other light weight fabric. Evening dresses are frequently described as being made of tarleton, but it was a different material then our present day fabric of the same name.

#22 - MASQUERADE COSTUME.  The original doll wardrobe that I studied in preparation for this Booklet had the most fetching little mask. So I did some research and concluded that fancy dress balls were a common occurrence—hence this outfit.  Make of black velvet the bodice according to the pattern given for the Ball Gown #23.  Trim the top with a ruffle of black lace.  Make the little bolero of rose pink velvet trimmed with blue velvet ribbon.  Make the tunic the same as the Ball dress tunic, of black lace, trimmed with a ruffle of narrow black lace and pink flowers and blue ribbons.  The blue skirt should be made according to the regular skirt pattern and trimmed around the bottom with two rows of black lace, again trimmed with blue ribbons and pink flowers.  Place a pink flower at center front of the bodice and in the doll's hair.  Add a black lace ruffle to hair, as a comb.  This, according to a fashion magazine of the time, represents a Spanish Dancer.

Sew the shoulder seams of the bolero.  Gather the top of the sleeves to fit the armcye and sew in place.  Gather and bind the bottom of the sleeves. Sew the under arm seams.  Pipe the raw edges of the bolero.  Sew pearls or small beads along the edge, and sew narrow ribbon as shown on pattern.

NOTE: Most of the sleeves and many of the seams were put in with piping during this period. In order to do this, make the piping and baste it to the sleeve on the seam line.  Cut a bias strip of fabric and double it over cording.  Machine stitch to hold cording in place.  Then proceed to set in the sleeve by top stitching in the crevice between piping and sleeve to the armcye.  The same rule applies to the other seams - baste the piping to one of the seam lines and sew the seam over it.  One thing to remember, and I quote from a periodical of the time, "If it is not stitched very close, the piping will look very loose and untidy."

-20-

#23 - <u>BALL DRESS.</u>  Make this of lavender silk or satin and trim it with lace or tulle.  If you use tulle, you should make a narrow hem in the bottom of all the ruffles.  Make the skirt according to directions. Trim the bottom of the three front gores with a ruffle of lace or tulle 2 1/4" wide.  Place a series of similar ruffles up the skirt as shown in the picture.  These ruffles should be about 1/2" wide.  Trim the outside curve of the train with a double ruffle.  Line the train with batiste. Slash the back of the train to the dot and hem for placket.  Gather the top of the train on the double dotted lines and draw up to fit the back of the skirt at the waist band.  Matching the two placket openings, turn under the raw edges of the train and slip stitch to the skirt at the waist band. The train should come far enough around the skirt to cover the edges of the ruffles in the front, as shown.  Line the tunic with batiste.  Sew the center back seam and hem placket opening.  Gather on triple dotted lines and draw up to 1".  Trim as in the sketch with a ruffle to match the train. Gather along the double dotted lined and draw up to fit the waist.  Pull most of the fullness to the back and sew to a cotton tape waistband. Close with a hook and eye.  Line the bodice with batiste.  Sew the darts in the front.  Sew the side backs to the center back and sew the shoulder seams.  Pipe the armcyes and sew the under arm seams.  Make the hem in the center backs and pipe the neckline and the bottom of the bodice.  Trim the neck with a double ruffle and a row of very narrow lace. The narrow lace should be tacked to the underside of the neck line so that just a little of it shows above the decollete.  Trim the dress with tiny roses or other small flowers as shown in the picture.  If your doll has cloth and porcelin arms, you may add the sleeves of the Evening Dress, #21, trimmed to match the neckline.

#24 - <u>WEDDING DRESS.</u>  Make this one of white or cream colored silk satin.  Work the pattern out in muslin first to make sure you have lengthened the skirt enough.  Then line the satin with batiste.  Sew the darts in the fronts.  Sew the side back pieces to the center back.  Slash center back to dot.  Turn under on dotted lines and hem back placket.  Make the inverted box pleats in the center back.  Tack in place.  Sew shoulder and under arm seams, making indicated tucks in side back pieces.  Using the sleeve pattern for the Evening Dress, #21, sew the sleeves together and set into the armcyes.  Pipe the neck, bottom of sleeves, and the bottom of the skirt.  Cut a piece of net or tulle a little wider than the front gore (at the bottom) and about **twice** as long as the front gore to the waist line.  Edge the bottom with 1/2" lace.  Run shirring threads and tack the panel to the front of the skirt, with the bottom about 1/2" from the bottom of the skirt, and the center top at the waist line.  Sew to the dress over the shirring lines as far as the solid lines on the skirt front. Trim away excess at the curved lines. Sew 3/4" lace around the neck and down the front, with the bottom of the lace on the curved line. Conceal the raw edges of the tulle with the bottom of the lace. Mitre the corners on the front gore.  When you reach the side seam, mitre the corner and continue the lace down to the bottom of the shirring and then around the back of the skirt. Place a band of the lace around the sleeves, whipping the lace to the top of the piping.  Trim the sleeve bottom and the neckline with a ruffle of 1/2" lace.  Make a fringed bow as you did for the Afternoon Dress, #17, and place across the back as shown, holding in place with small snaps. Close the back with concealed hooks and eyes.  Trim with small flowers or bows.  Sew two pieces of cotton tape to side seams at tucks (underside) and tie in back to pull skirt fullness to back.

Make the veil of a circle of tulle trimmed as shown with small flowers.

# WRAPS

    **#25 - DOLMAN.** Make of light weight wool and line with silk. The original was white wool with dull orange embroidery and white silk fringe. Sew the center back seam. Sew the shoulder seams. Gather the tops of the sleeves along the double dotted lines and draw up so that the dots in front and back match. Sew sleeve sections to front and backs. Turn back front facings and sew in place. Bind bottom edges all the way around. Sew the collar front edges, turn, and sew collar to neck. Face the raw edges. Trim all outside edges and all seams with embroidery as shown. Trim the bottom with fringe, if you have some, or lace, 1 1/2" wide. Sew a piece of cotton tape, long enough to go around dolls waist, to the seams on the underside. This is to make sure that the sleeve fullness stays over the sleeve arms. There is no front closing.

    **#26 - PALETOT.** Make this of a deep colored velvet and omit lining. Sew the center back seam and sew the back side pieces to the back. Sew the shoulder seams. Draw sleeves up along double dotted lines and sew to armcyes. Sew under arm seams. Turn under front facing and hem in place. Bind collar narrowly with silk and sew in place, facing raw edge of neck on the inside with silk. Bind all other raw edges with silk and trim with a ruffle of 3/4" black lace. Close front with concealed hooks and eyes and place a silk bow at center front. The silk binding and bow may either match or contrast with the velvet.

    **#27 - HOOD.** Make of lightweight wool and line with silk. Make double box pleats at center back. Sew together at neck and cover with a small bow. Gather top front along double dotted lines slightly. Cover these stitches with another small bow, this time with streamers hanging down the back. Bind all outside edges and trim with six strand embroidery floss couched in the design shown. Close front under chin with another bow.

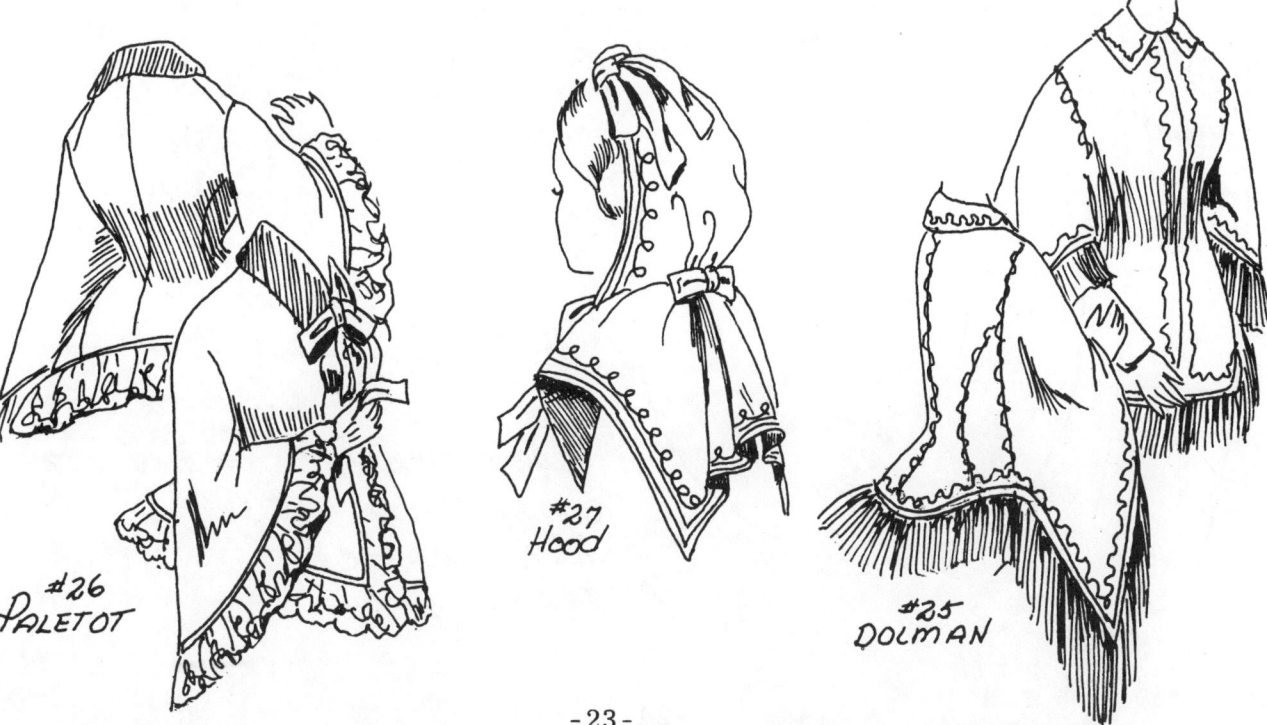

#28 - <u>HATS.</u> This is the same method for making hats as described in Volume II. Since I have discovered no better way to make them, I repeat it here. Cut both the pattern parts of some light weight card. Using scotch or masking tape, fasten the parts together right on the edges. You won't have to overlap, so no seam allowances are given. Now, get yourself a cup of warm water, a needle and thread, and straw. Coil the straw in the cup of water. Let it soften a minute. Beginning at the outside edges, start sewing the straw round and round, overlaping the straw slightly and whipping the rounds together. Do not sew the straw and the cardboard together. If you find it difficult to keep the outside round in place, baste it to the cardboard. Keep the straw in the water so that it will remain as flexible as possible. Keep sewing round and round up the crown. When you reach the top, make a little circle of straw for the top of the crown. Now dampen the whole thing again. Turn the brim up or down, according to the hat you are making. Place the bonnet on a thread spool and hold the brim in place with rubber bands or temporary basting until it is dry. Set aside and dry thoroughly. When it is dry, remove the basting stitches from the outside round, and the bonnet from the form. The hat may be trimmed according to any of the pictures in the booklet with flowers, ribbons, and feathers. For cloth hats, use the same pattern, make a base of buckram or card, and cover with flowers.

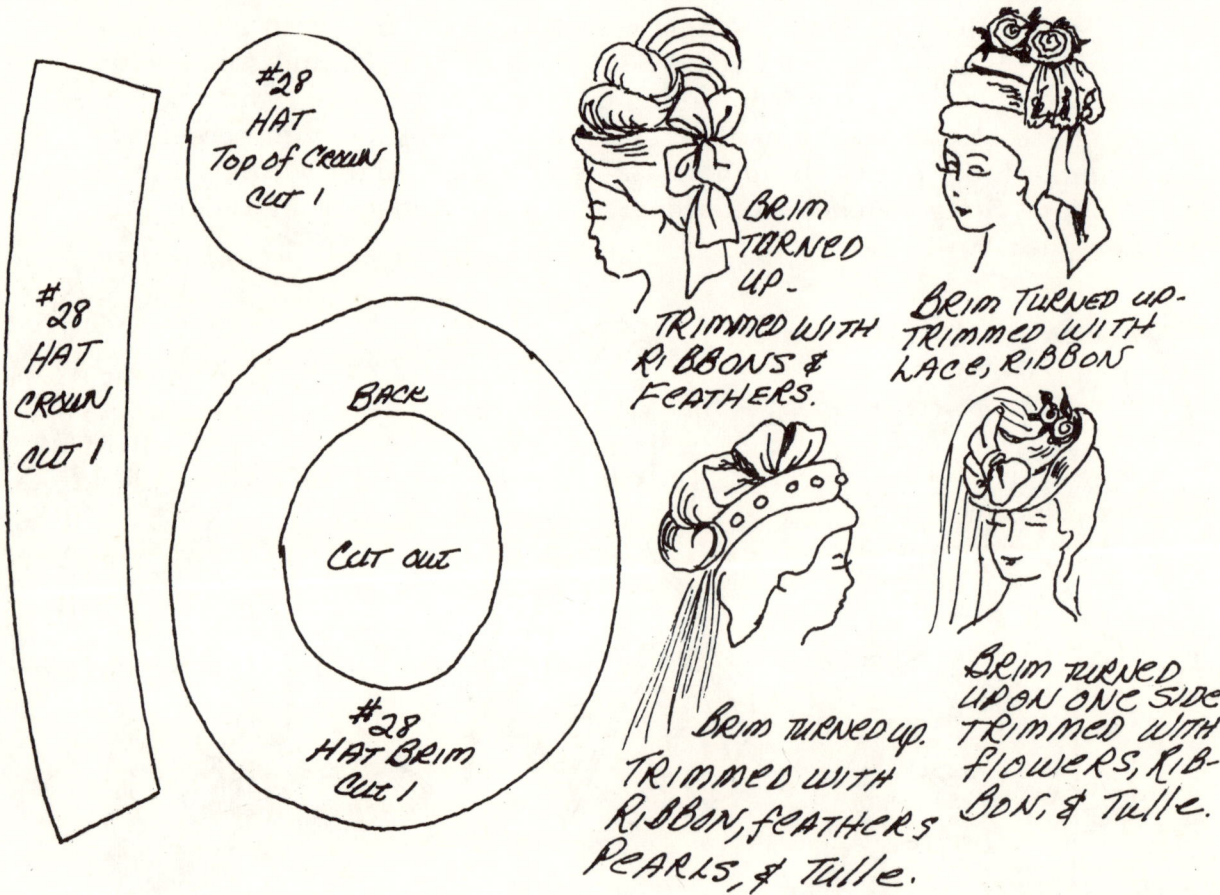

## ACCESSORIES

**#29 - APRON.** Make of batiste or fine linen. Sew the side gores to the center front gore of the skirt. Turn a very narrow hem and whip a narrow lace ruffle all the way around the outside edge. Sew to a narrow waistband long enough to go around the doll's waist and close with a button and loop. Make a narrow hem in the top and edge the hem with lace. Sew to the waistband. Use sequin pins to fasten to the dress over which it is to be worn.

**#30 - JABOT.** Cut a piece of fine lace or batiste 9" long and 1" wide. Make a narrow hem on all sides with mitred points at each end. Trim the pointed ends with narrow lace ruffles. Tie around doll's neck in a bow.

**#31 - HANDKERCHIEF.** Cut a two inch square of batiste or linen. Make a narrow hem on all sides. You may either leave plain or, for more formal wear, trim with a narrow lace ruffle. The most patient among you may want to embroider the doll's initial on one corner.

**#32 - COLLAR AND CUFFS.** These may also be made of batiste or linen. Make a narrow hem along the dotted lines. Narrowly bind along the solid lines and close with a button and loop. Again, these may be trimmed with a ruffle of narrow lace. NOTE: The Jabot, and the collar and cuffs are designed to be worn wherever they seem to fit. They are items which seem to be included in great abundance in all French Fashion Doll wardrobes.

**#33 - TOWELS AND WASHCLOTHS.** Make these of a fairly heavy (in a doll sense) linen. Cut the washcloths 2" by 2". Fringe the edges to a depth of 1/4". Cut the towels 4" by 8". Hem, narrowly, the long edges, and fringe the short ones to a depth of 1".

**#34 - TOOTHBRUSH.** Carve the toothbrush out of the wide end of a flat toothpick. Use a sliver of white fur or white felt for the bristles.

**#35 - MIRROR.** Carve the mirror of 1/4" Balsa, bass or plywood. Sand all edges and surfaces to smoothness. Stain the wood mahogany. Cut a piece of foil paper to fit within the dotted lines and glue in place. If you wish, you may paint the doll's initials on the back of the mirror in gold.

**#36 - HAIRBRUSH.** Carve and stain as you did the mirror and of the same wood. As with the toothbrush, glue a piece of felt or fur in place for bristles. If you use white fur, you will have to trim it to a flat surface.

**#37 - MASK.** Cut the mask of heavy white paper. Glue, using Elmer's, to wrong side of fabric. Cut away excess fabric close to the paper. Trim the bottom with a black lace ruffle and sew narrow ribbon to x's.

**#38 - JEWELRY BOX.** Provide yourself with a pill box in a pretty design, either round, square, or oblong. Pad the inside with silk. NOTE: Pretty pillboxes are mostly found in gift and dime stores. In this day of all sorts of pills - you can find them almost anyplace.

#39 - <u>FAN.</u> In order to make my fan, I took apart a Japanese fan (doll sized) and replaced the gold and silver paper with lace. If you can't find one of the Japanese ones, cut the end sticks of 1/8" balsa or bass and the inside ones of flat toothpicks. Sand all pieces and paint the color you want. Punch the holes with a hot needle and thread together with a thin wire. Twist the end of the wire and bend into a circle. Cut the fan part of lace and glue to the sticks on shaded lines. Fold, fan fashion, and tie a narrow ribbon bow with long streamers to the wire loop.

#40 - <u>VALISE.</u> Cover the outside and one end of a match box (small size) with leather. Make the incised lines with a steel knitting needle or a leather decorating tool. Cut off the heads of small brass nails and glue in place as shown. Make the handles of narrow strips of the leather and glue in place. Cover one end of the inside of the match box with leather and the inside with a small cotton print. Make a little leather loop and glue it to the bottom of the inside of the box to pull it open.

#41 - <u>LAP ROBE.</u> Cut a piece of plaid wool 10" by 10". Make a one inch deep wool fringe all the way around the robe. Cut two narrow leather straps 8" long, and one 1/2" long. Make a loop at either end of the shorter piece and thread the longer ones through. Fasten the robe in the carrier with small wire buckles made as shown.

#42 - <u>GLOVES.</u> Since these small dolls have mitten hands, there is no point in trying to make gloves for them to wear. Cut the glove outline of felt or leather, bunch them up, and let the doll carry them.

#43 - <u>TRUNK.</u> Cut the pieces of the trunk of heavy cardboard. Glue together. Cover the outside with leather and line the inside with a small print. Glue two small pieces of wood to the indicated lines to support the tray. Make the tray of a lighter weight cardboard and glue together. Cover the whole thing with the small print. Glue narrow leather bands to the outside of the trunk as shown and fasten with wire buckles. Glue the handles in place, and trim trunk as shown, with small brass nailheads.

These are of course, only suggestions to get you started on the collection of goodies your doll should have to put in her trunk. Watch in the miniature lists, dime stores and gift shops for little items that you can get ready-made to complete the outfit for your Fashion Doll. Bead necklaces, scissors, a sewing basket, complete with pincushion and needle, hair pins and hair nets, calling cards, stationery - these are just a few suggestions of things the well dressed Fashion Doll of the 1870's might have had in her trousseau.

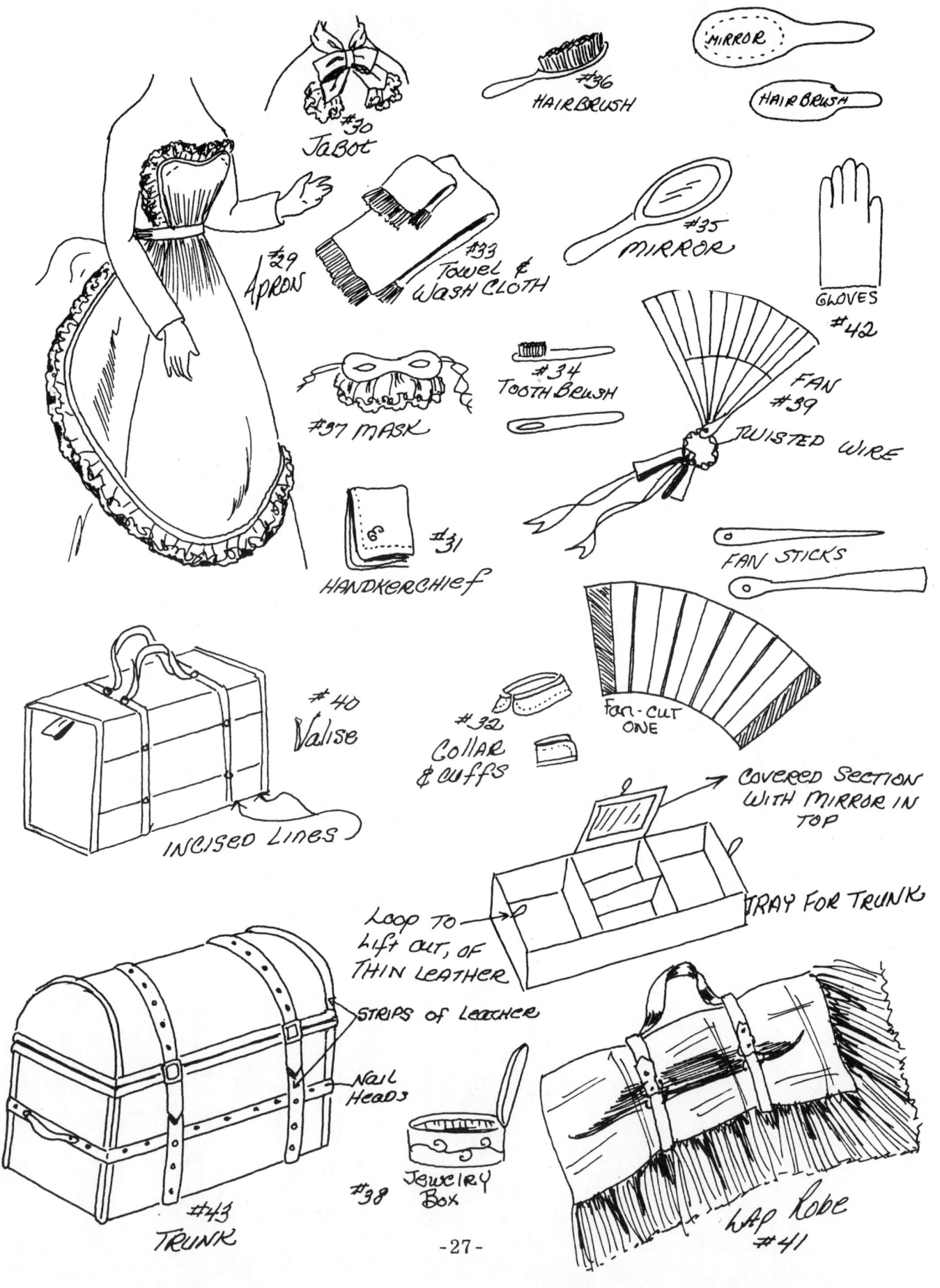

## THE PATTERNS

With the exception of just a few patterns already given, all of the patterns are on the following pages. When you are ready to make one of the garments, I suggest that you trace it out of the book onto light weight muslin, making note of all darts, notches, and other pertinent information. Then you may go right ahead and baste the pattern together to be sure that it fits just as you want it to. Then you can rip it apart and cut your fabric by the muslin. When you are through, you can place the pattern pieces into an envelope where they will be safe until the next time you need them. Please be sure when you are tracing the patterns that you get all the pieces to the garment you are working on.

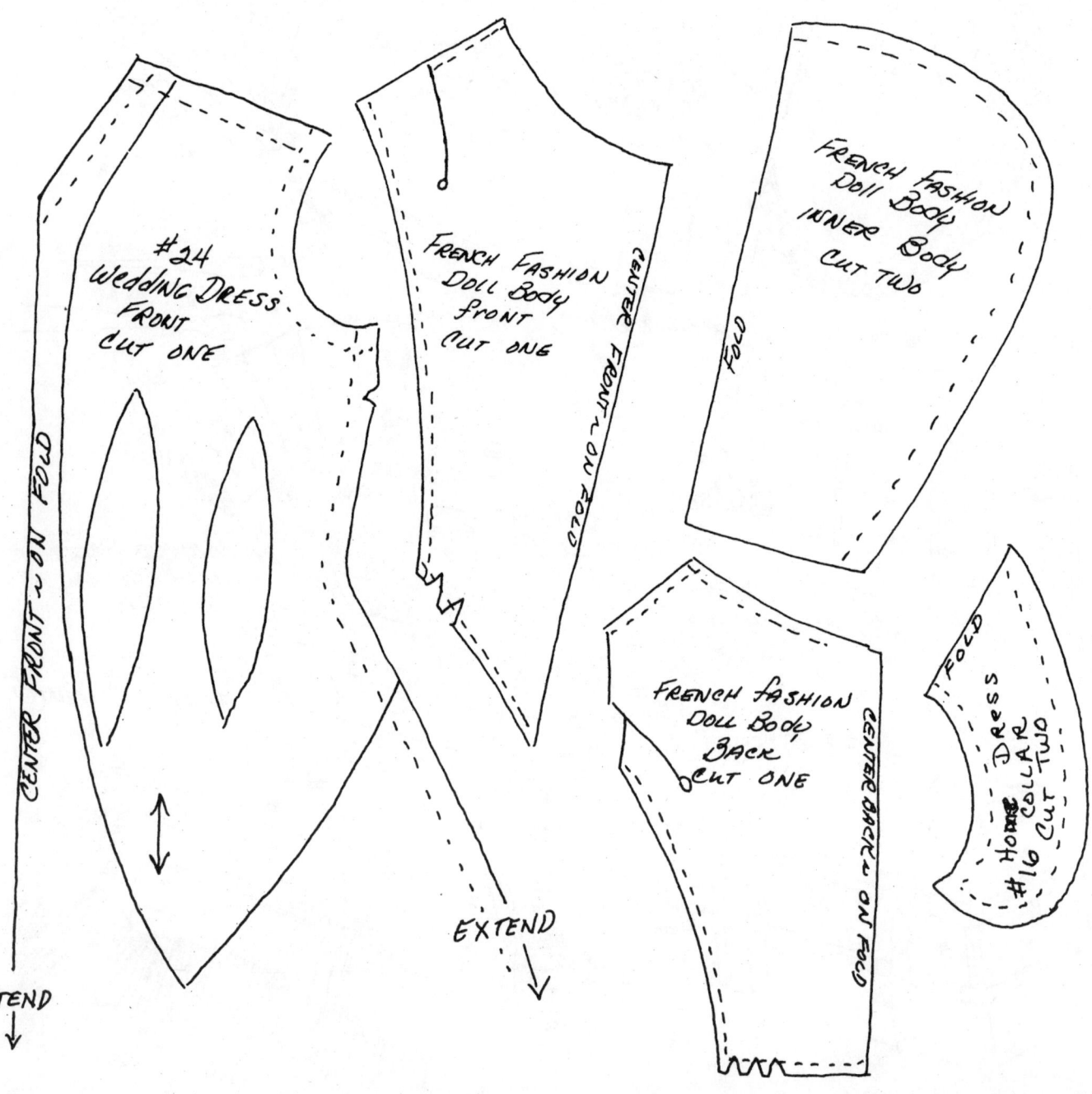

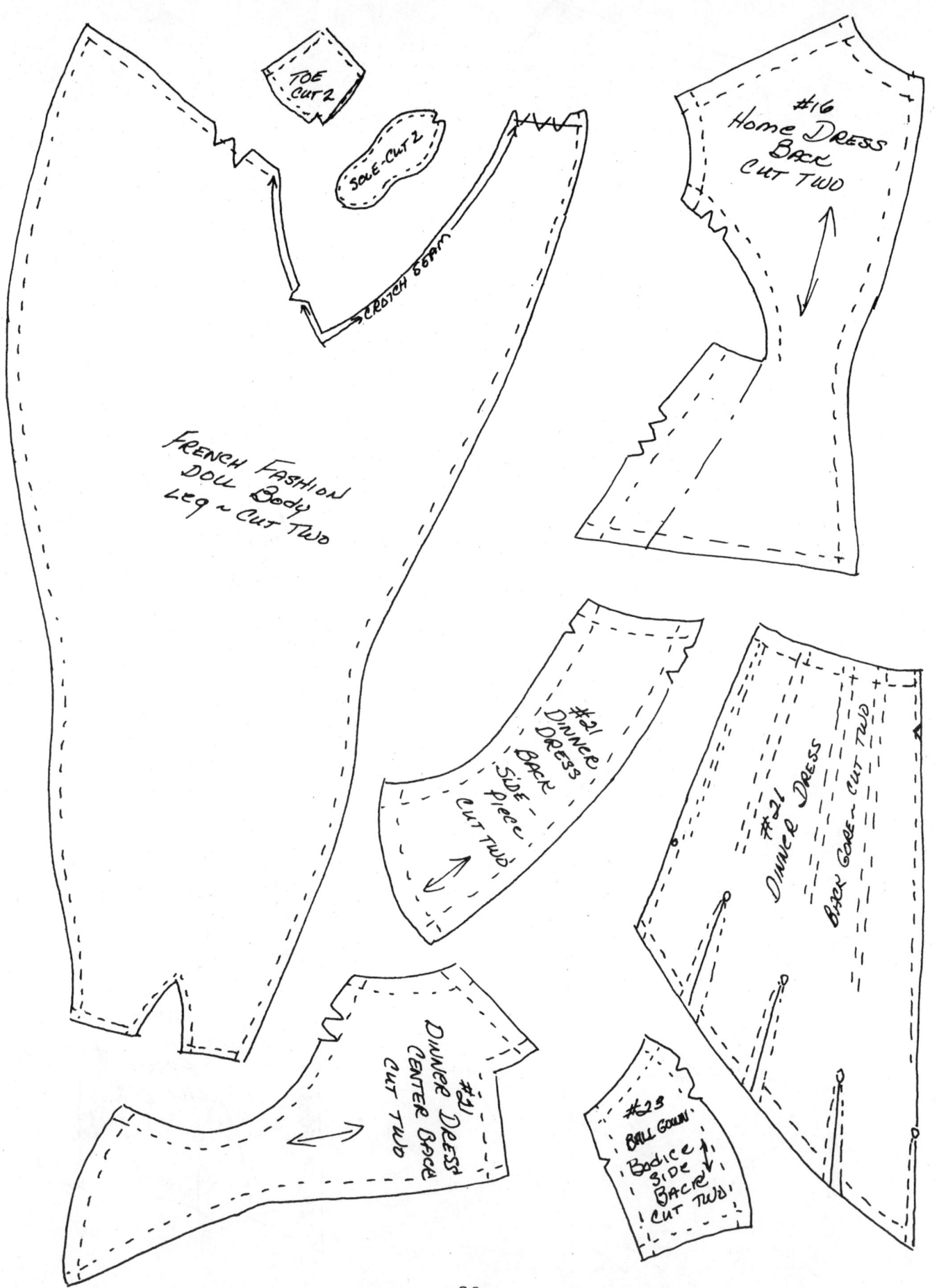

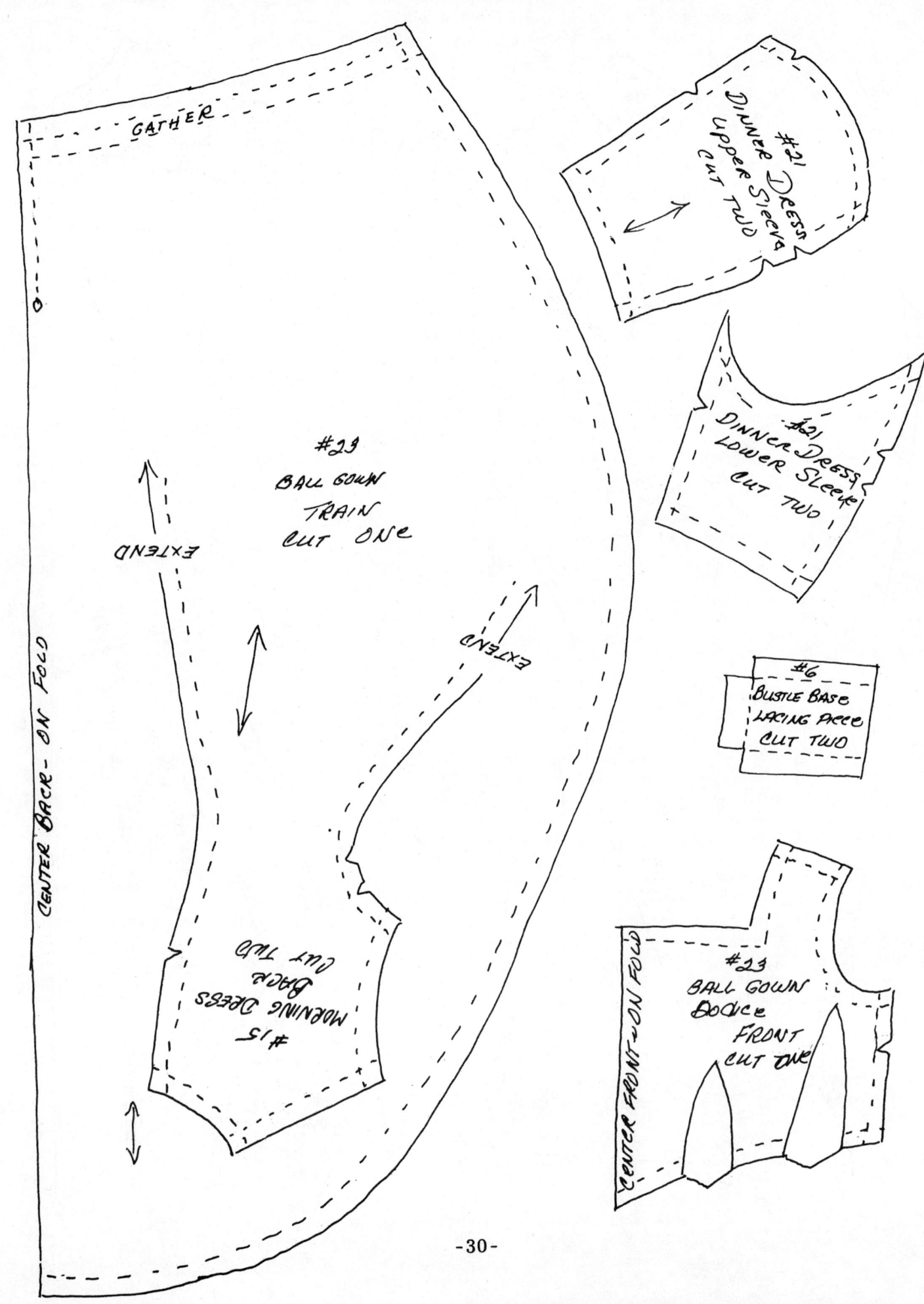

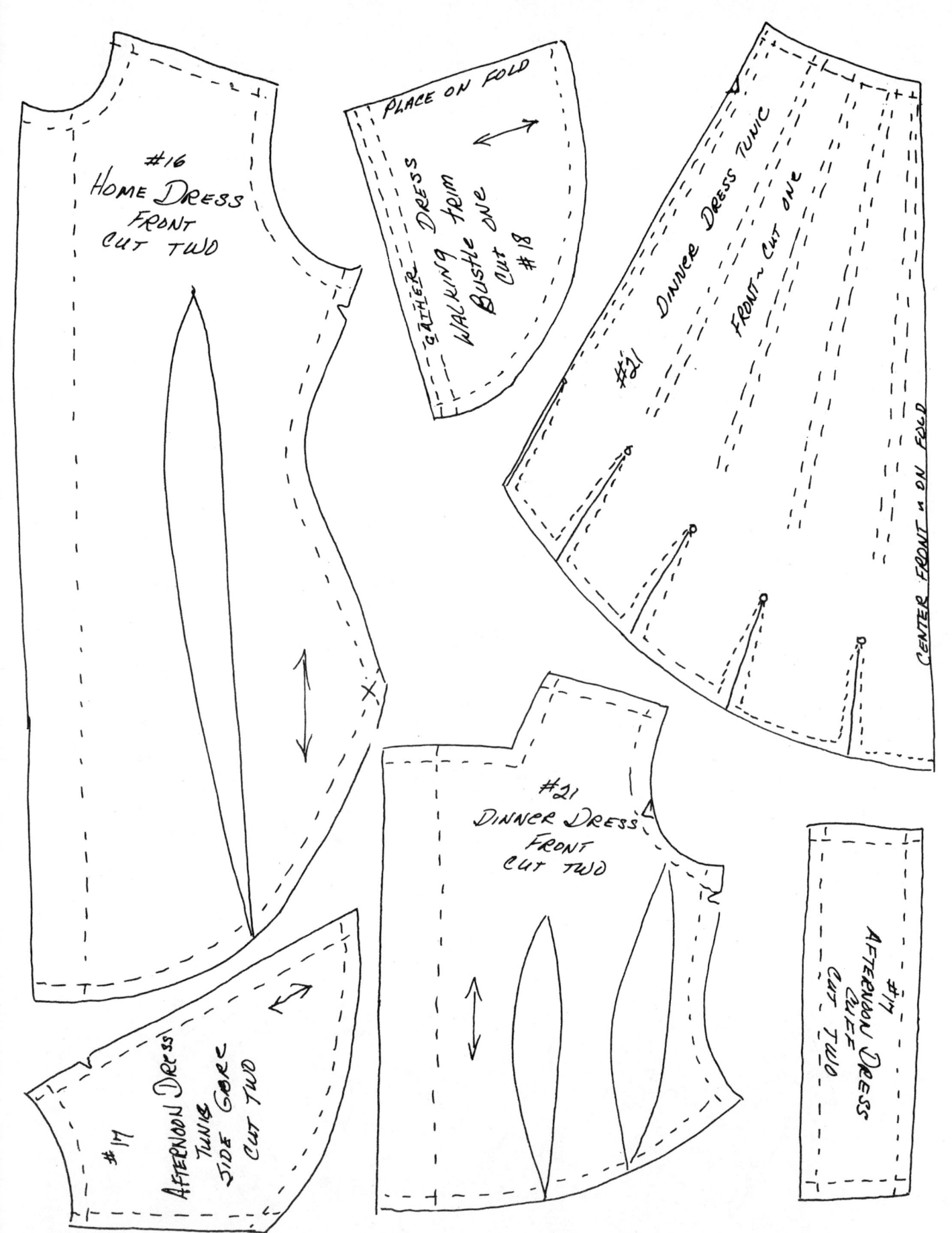

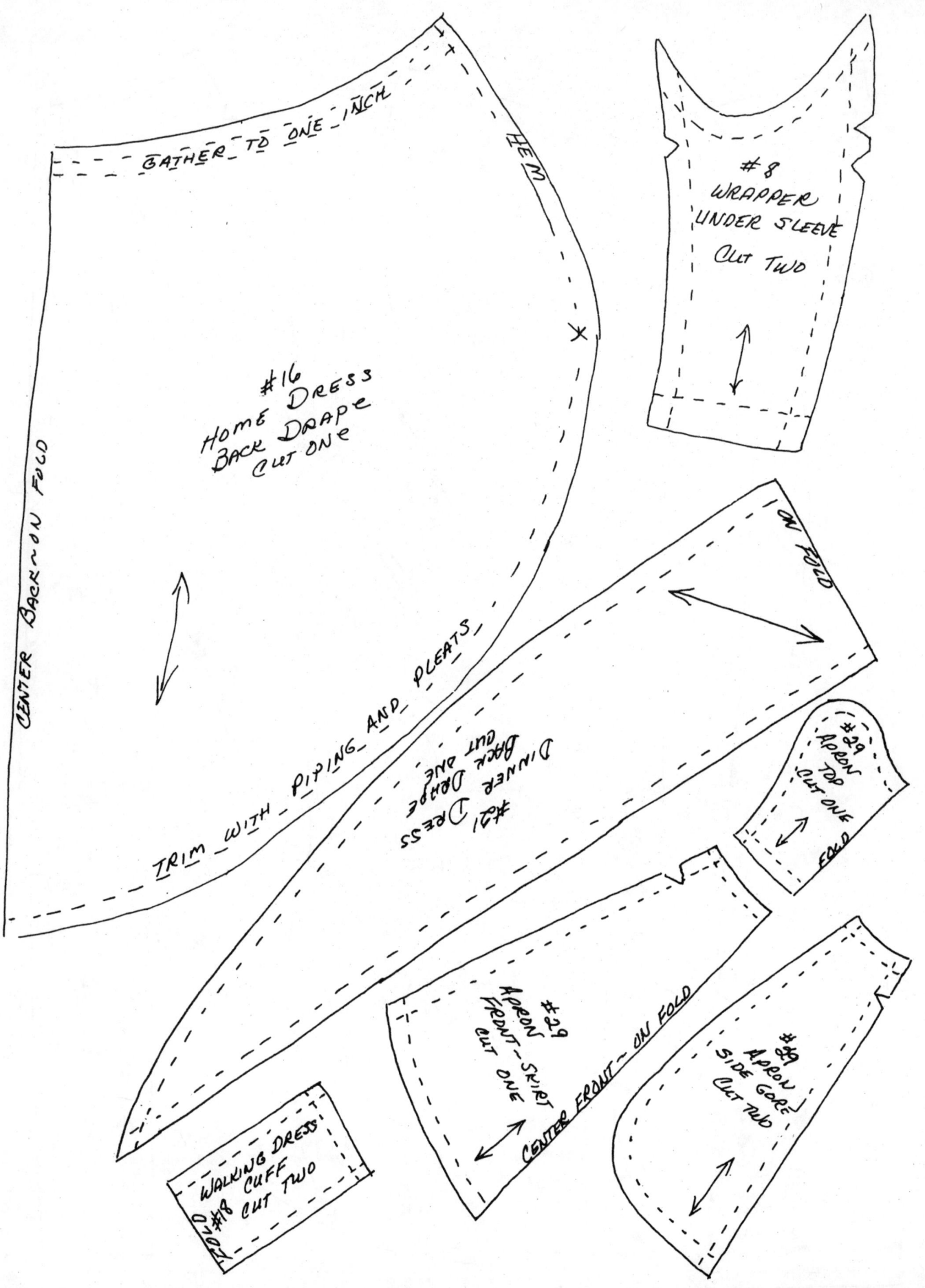

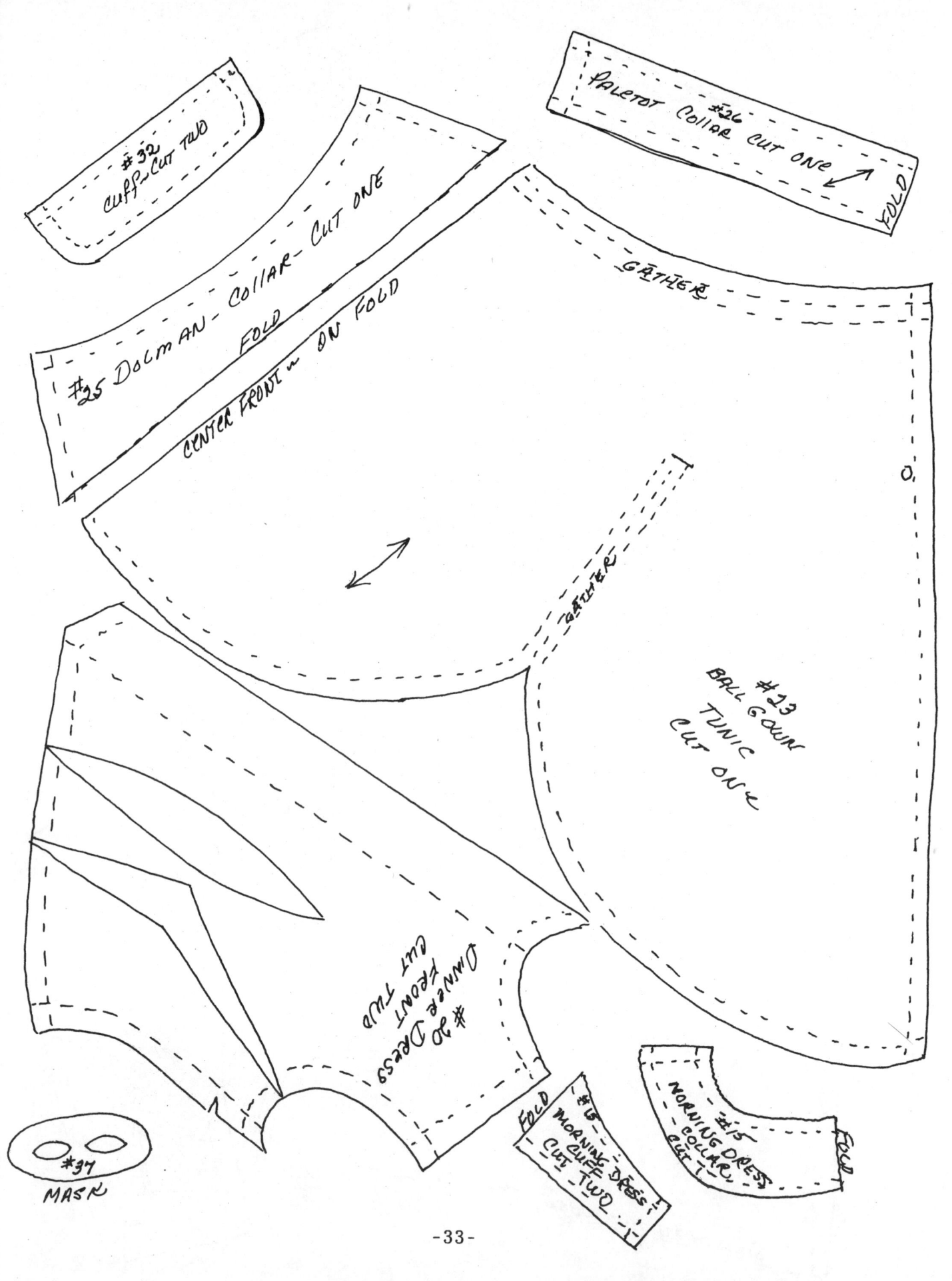

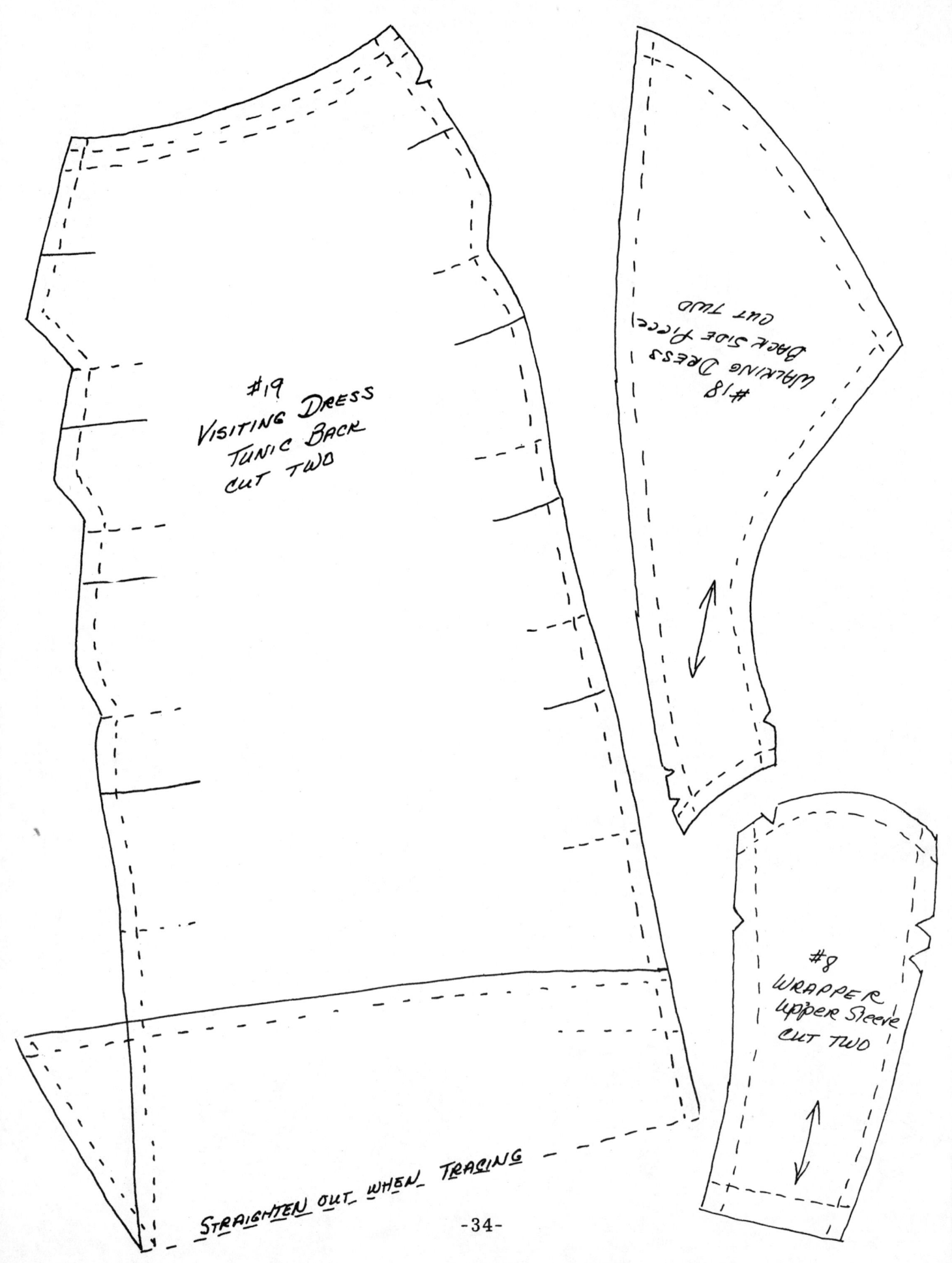

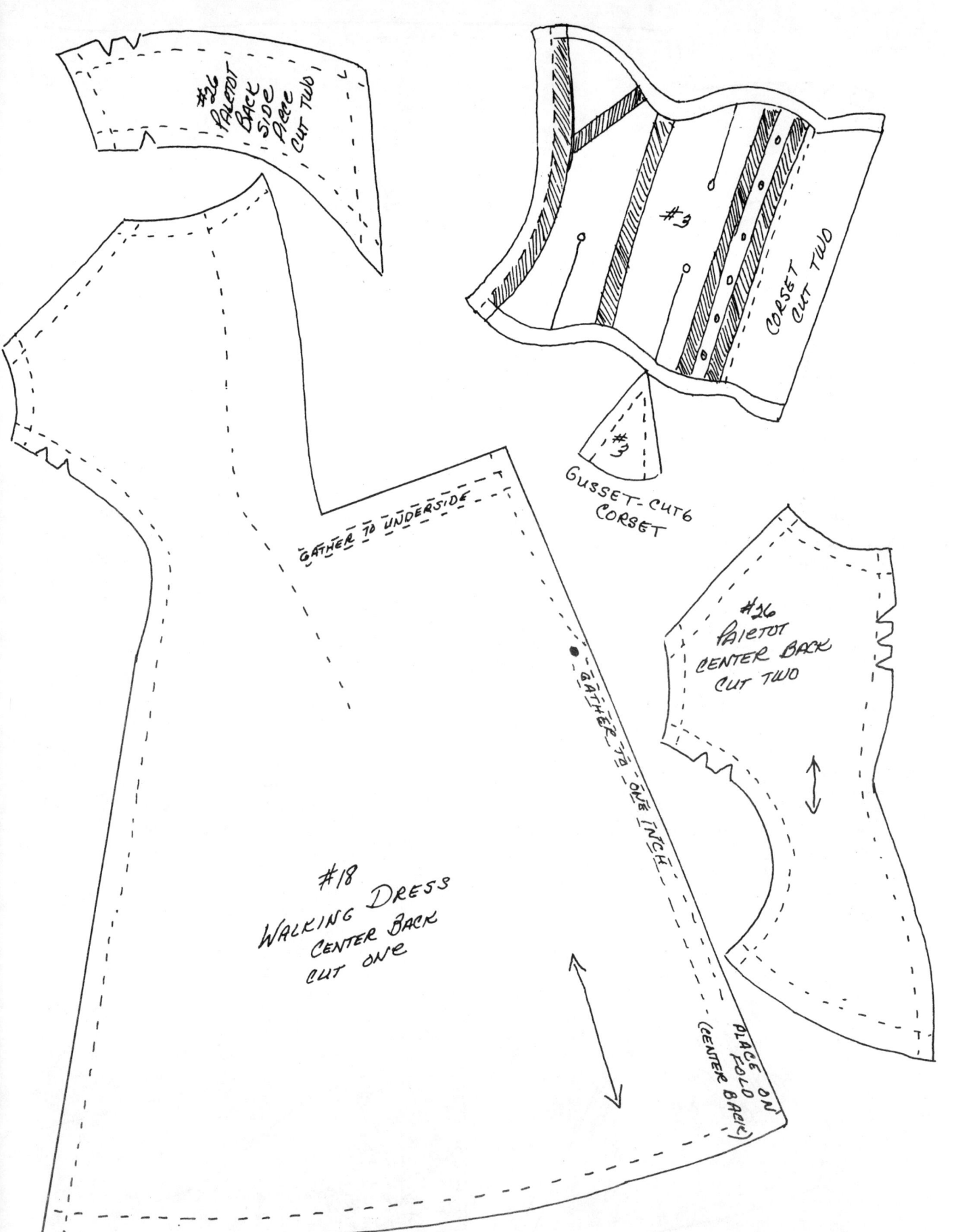

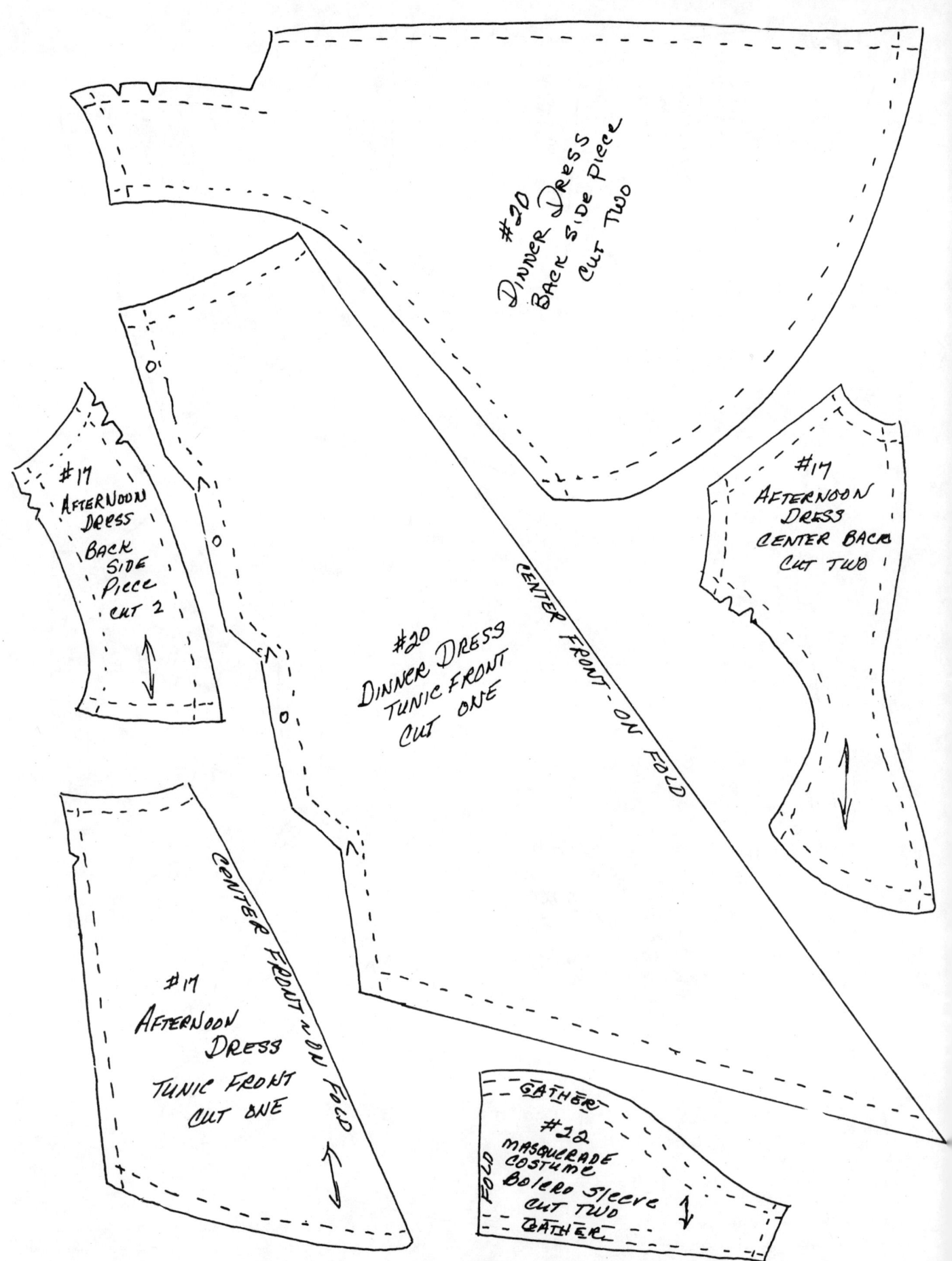

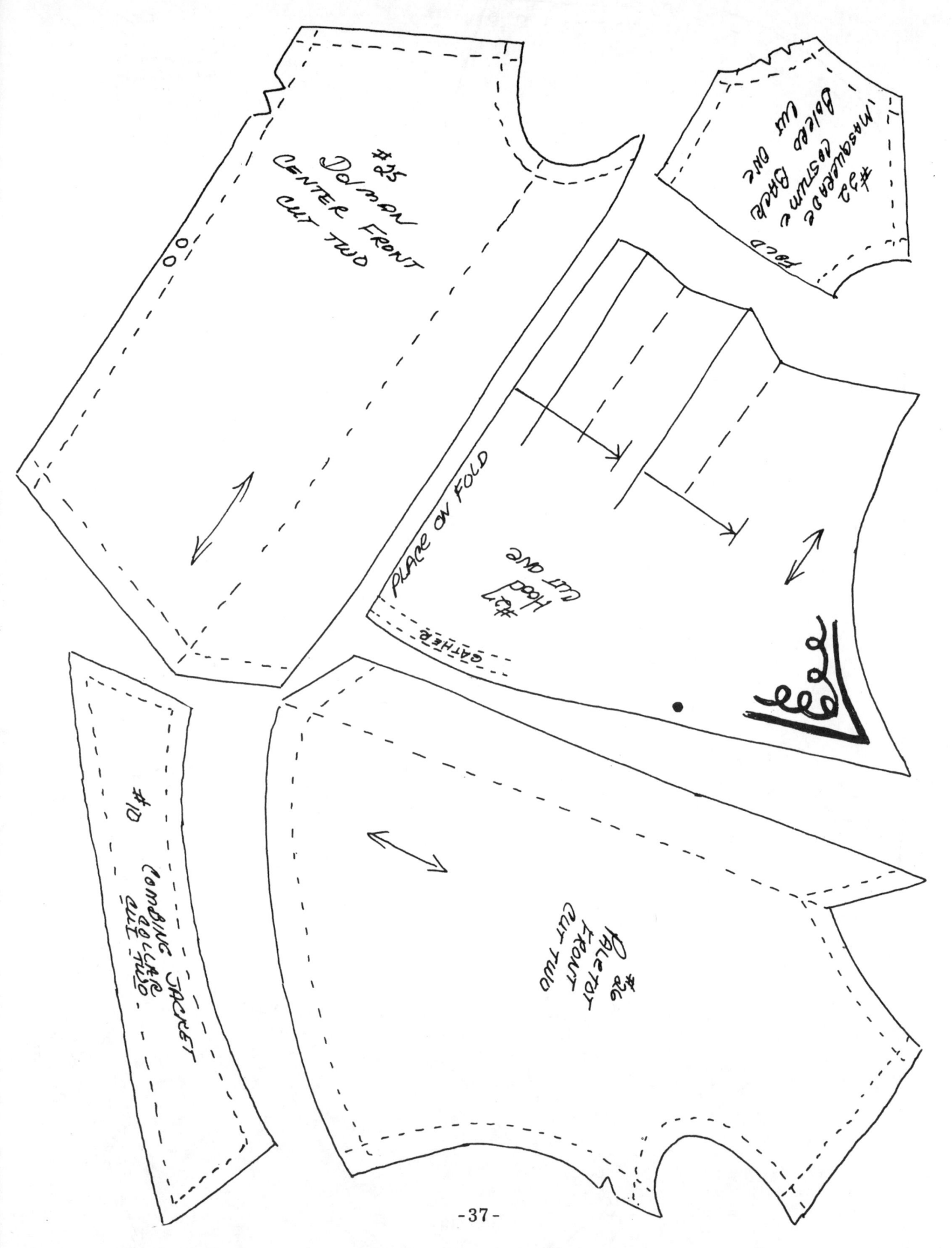

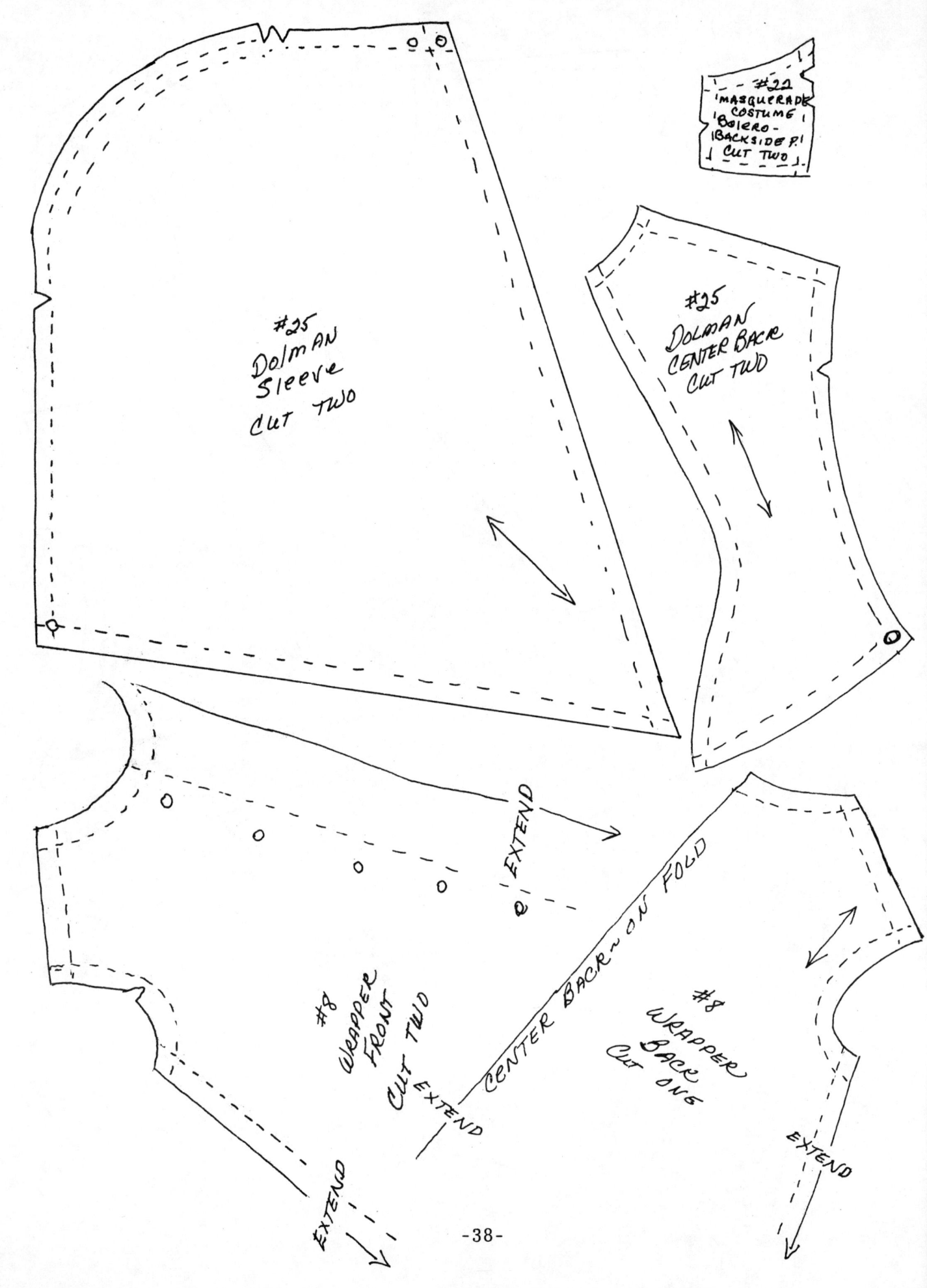

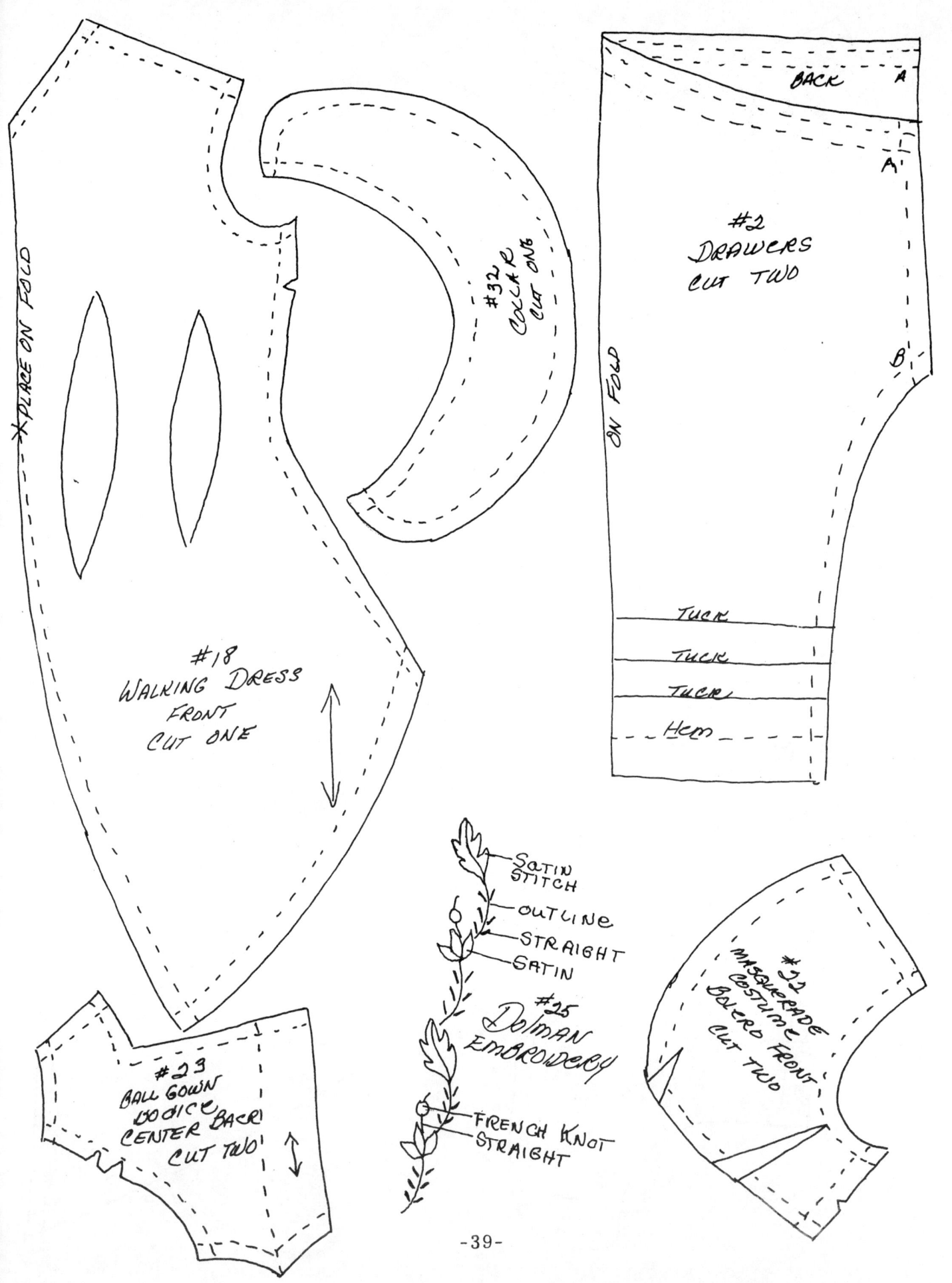

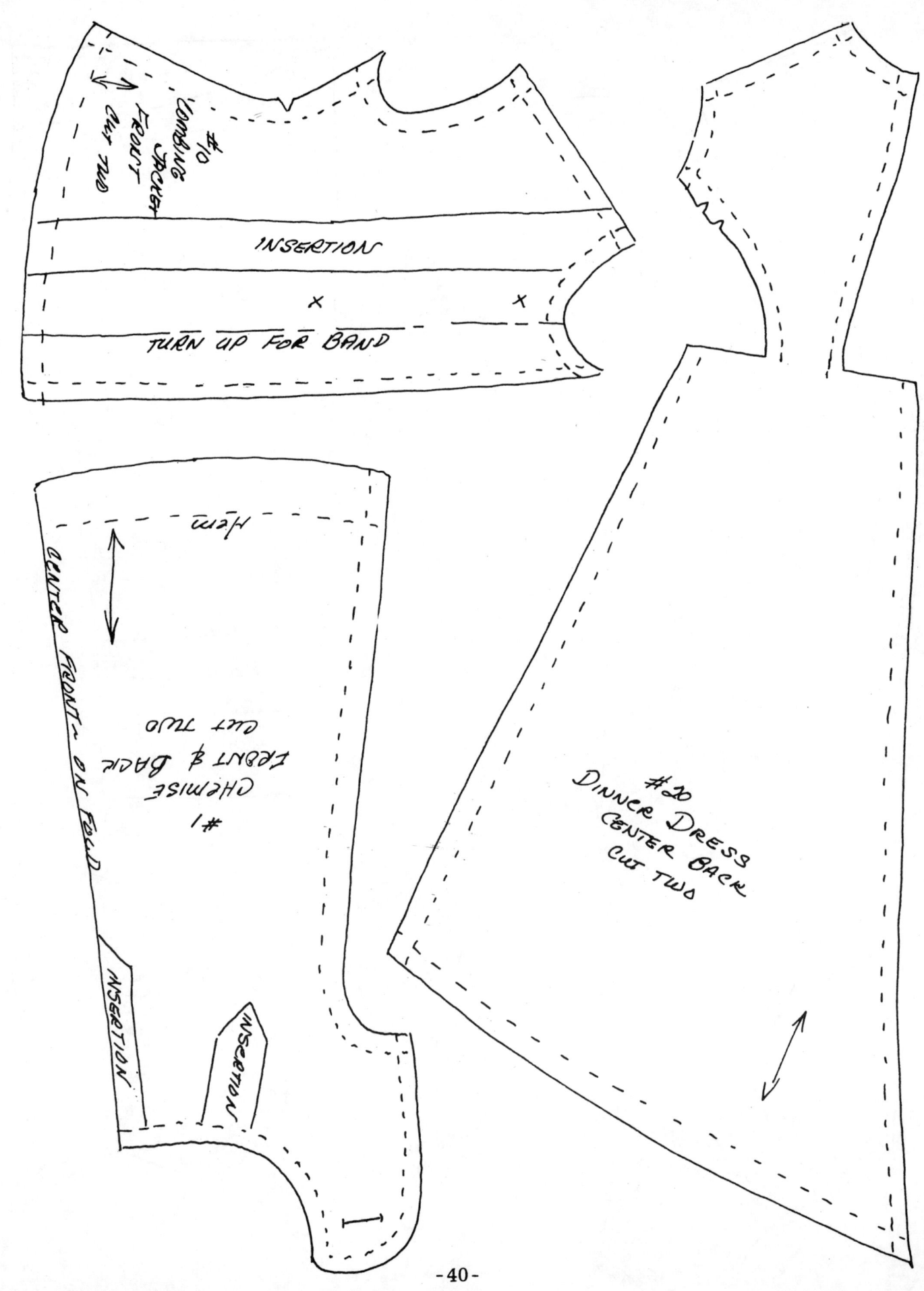

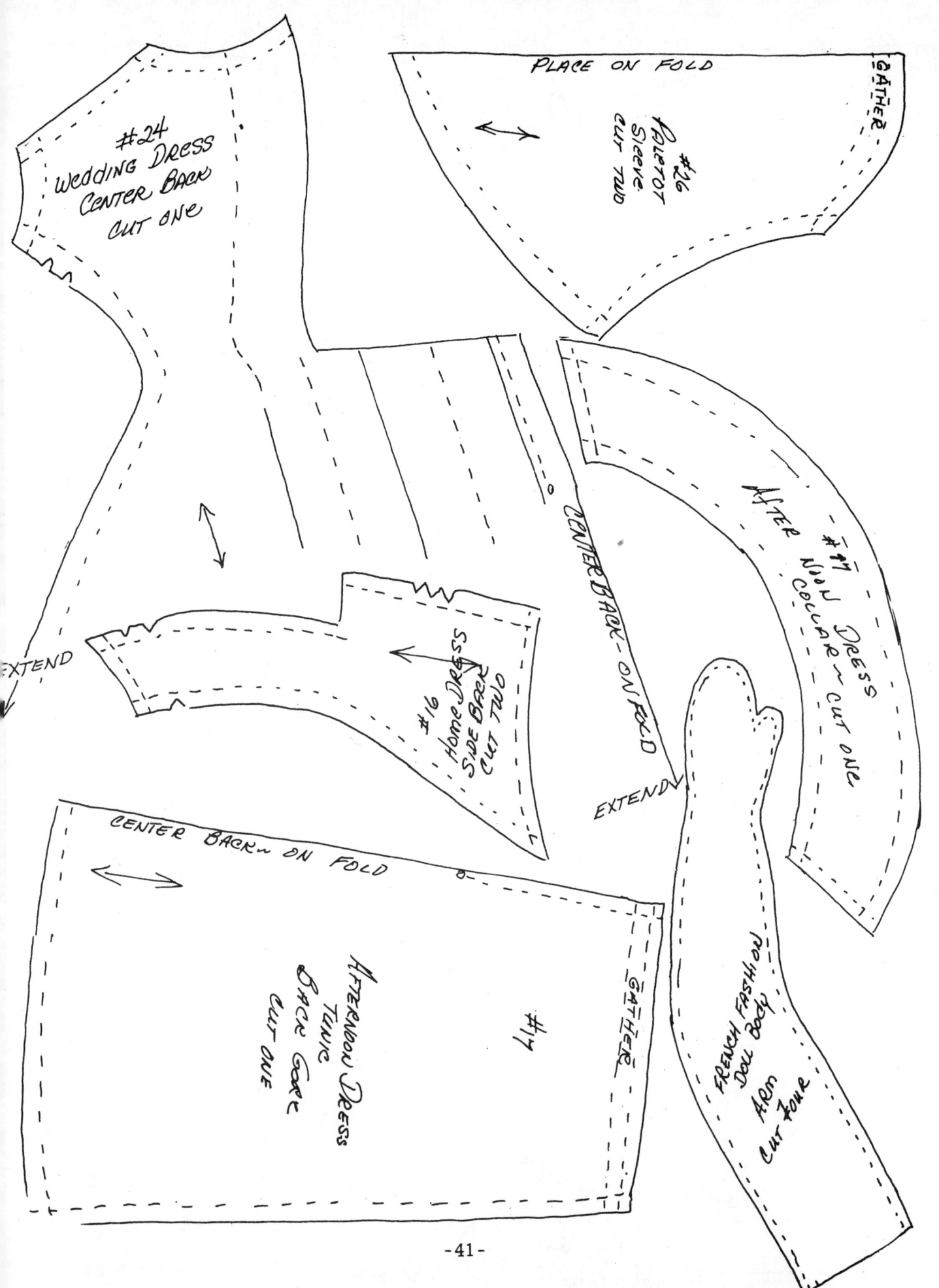

#4 Petticoat Front
Cut One
Center Front - on Fold
Hem
Ruffle

Skirt Back
Cut Two
Gather
Sew Casing Here
Extend if Necessary

#14 Skirt Side Gore
Cut Two

-43-

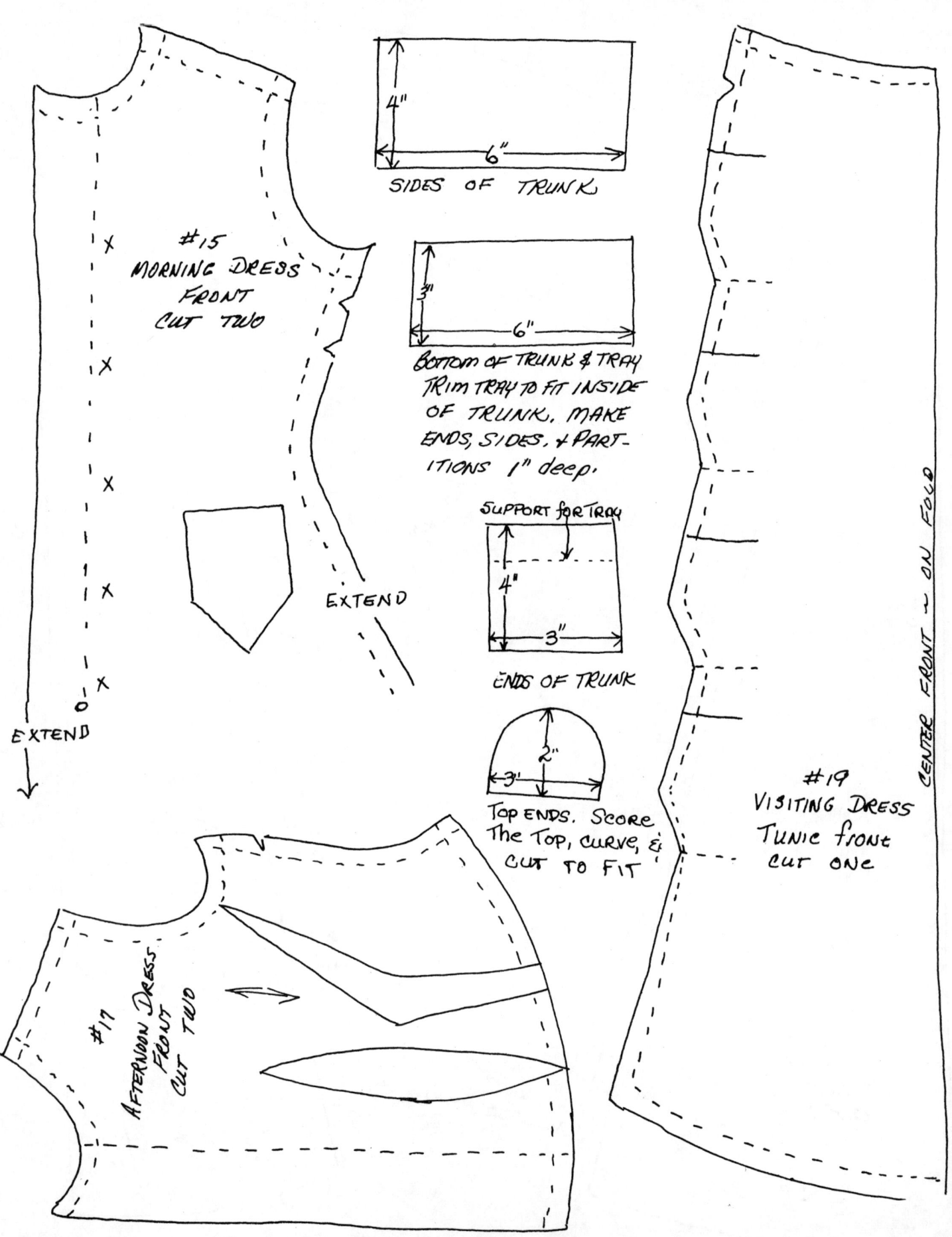

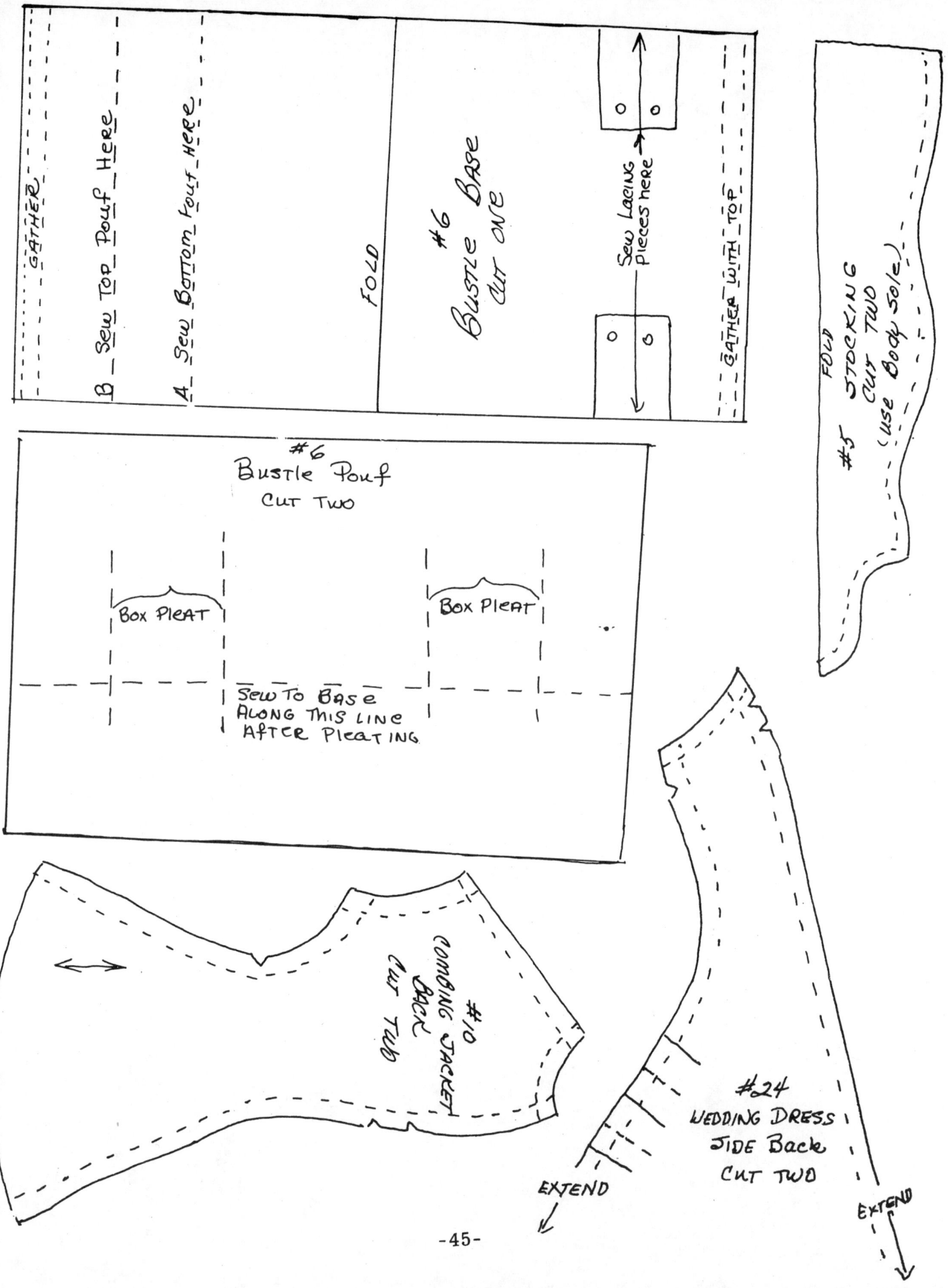